Prior Park

Cover illustrations
Front cover: Nelson print of Prior Park, from a lithograph of c.1860
Back cover: Late 19th century photograph of the Palladian Bridge and Mansion

Prior Park

A Compleat Landscape

Gillian Clarke

Millstream Books

For Susannah and Edward.

My sincere thanks are due to Chris Pound for his encouraging advice on the manuscript, and his help in preparing plans and drawings; likewise to Camilla Fitzgibbon who undertook some of the research and introduced me to many books and articles. To others I am also grateful: for the kind interest and help of Rev. J. A. Harding, Clifton Diocesan Archivist; for the enthusiastic comments of David McLaughlin and Peter Atkinson; for helpful discussion on geology with Diana Smith; and to Colin Johnson, City Archivist, and the staff of Bath Reference Library who provided source material quickly and efficiently. Finally, to Pat Baynes for typing the draft so patiently.

Photographs and illustrations are reproduced by permission of:-

Bodleian Library – MS. Gough a.4 fol.63 – (p. 36)
Royal Commission on the Historical Monuments of England
Victoria Art Gallery, Bath City Council
Bath Reference Library
Adrian Stride
The Courtauld Institute of Art, Conway Library
Taunton Local History Library
Clifton Diocesan Archives
Katy Duke
Chris Pound
David McLaughlin

First Published 1987

Millstream Books
7 Orange Grove
Bath
Avon BA1 1LP

This book is set in 11 on 13 point Baskerville
Typeset by Character Graphics, Taunton
Cover printed by Matthews Wright, Chard
Printed in Great Britain by Netherwood Dalton & Co., Huddersfield

© Gillian Clarke 1987

ISBN 0948975067

Contents

	Prologue	Page 7
Chapter One	Works and Inventions	Page 9
Chapter Two	Like the Stages of a Roman Theatre	Page 17
Chapter Three	A Devotion to Antiquity	Page 23
Chapter Four	A Pretty Landskip	Page 31
Chapter Five	Mr. Allen's Gardens	Page 41
Chapter Six	Surveying and Making Plans	Page 51
Chapter Seven	Perhaps the Finest View in the Kingdom	Page 61
Chapter Eight	For All Bath to See	Page 71
	Epilogue	Page 78
	Bibliography	Page 79
	Index	Page 80

The view northwards from the steps of the mansion

Prologue

The grounds at Prior Park epitomise the English Landscape Garden of the mid-eighteenth century. It is one of the few gardens where Alexander Pope is known to have had some influence in the design, and which survives to this day. 'Capability' Brown may also have worked here; even if he did not, his style of landscaping was introduced.

John Wood planned the building of Prior Park with the view very much in mind, and this has proved to be the major success of the design. James Tunstall, writing his *Rambles about Bath* in 1847, spoke for many visitors past and present when he said it is "a more beautiful and varied view than any other private residence in the kingdom, embracing an extensive prospect".

Unlike many of England's country houses, Prior Park was the creation of a self-made business man, Ralph Allen, and was not the estate of a centuries-old landed family. Its existence could so easily have been jeopardised by the multiplicity of owners and tenants that followed. In part, it was rescued and revitalised in the nineteenth century by Bishop Baines, who set the course for education at Prior Park.

In spite of its many guardians, the same landscape, and very nearly the same buildings, have been retained, sometimes enhanced, and have even decayed, but have not been radically altered in 250 years.

Prior Park is listed Grade 1 on the Historic Buildings and Monuments Commission Register of Historic Parks and Gardens.

An engraving of Prior Park by Anthony Walker, c. 1754

1 – Works and Inventions

When Ralph Allen came to Bath in 1710, it had a population of little more than two thousand and was still a small town contained by its wall; however, it must have engendered a certain air of excitement and distinction. The unique hot springs attracted a number of famous and distinguished visitors, including royalty, to Bath. In the 17th century, Anne of Denmark and Catherine of Braganza visited the city as did Princess Anne, who returned later in 1702 and 1703 as Queen. Bath was fast becoming a resort where bathing, 'taking the waters' and meeting others of the most fashionable sort were the main attractions. It had been a famous Roman town and anyone of classical persuasion would have appreciated, in this English Augustan period, the prospects for re-building the city. Development was inevitable.

The life and career of Ralph Allen have been excellently documented elsewhere and there is no need to repeat the events of his life in depth.[1] However, it is worth reminding ourselves of Allen's progress as a young lad, born into a modest home in St. Columb Major parish, Cornwall, in 1693, from where he moved to Exeter in 1708 and then on to Bath.

Ralph Allen had helped his family in the Post Office at St. Columb, had probably worked in Exeter Post Office, and in 1712 became deputy-postmaster in Bath. In 1719, Allen made a proposal to the government to take over, reorganise and manage the service of Cross-Road and Bye Posts at some financial risk to himself. Starting in 1720, through hard work, Allen was eventually able to show a profit on the operation. It was as the efficient operator of this system of letter posts that Allen amassed his first fortune. In 1721, he married a London girl, Elizabeth Buckeridge, although there is little information or comment about his first wife.[2] His brother-in-law, Anthony Buckeridge, Esq. of Ware, is said to have promised substantial assistance as well as a dowry which must have helped in financing the cross-posts project.

Already Allen was beginning to form the political allegiances which were to guide his taste and his opinions in the years to come. Of importance was Major-General George Wade, who was commemorated later with a statue in the deer park of Prior Park. He was involved in quelling a Jacobite uprising

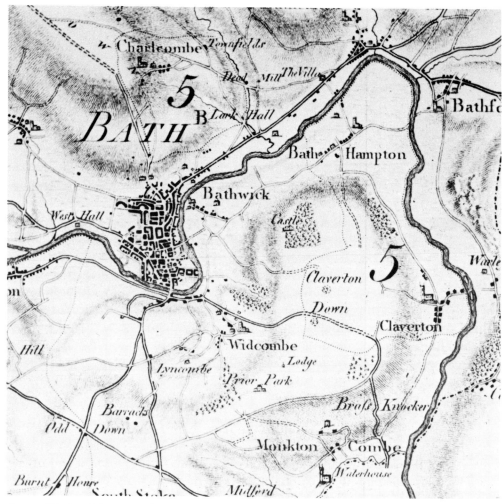

A map of Bath and the surrounding area in 1782, by Day and Masters

in 1715 in the neighbourhood of Bath when Allen is reputed to have acted as informant. Richard Graves, writing his *Trifling Anecdotes* in 1806, says that Allen:

> *having got intelligence of a waggon load of arms, which was coming up from the West, for the use of the disaffected in this part of England . . . communicated this to General Wade: who was then quartered with troops at Bath.*[3]

Wade duly dispatched these enemies of the King and, thus indebted to Allen, helped establish the latter's name and fortune. Richard Jones, in his autobiography, states that Wade acted as "bond-man" to the Government when in 1720, Allen won his first bid to secure from the Postmaster General a large contract for the Cross-Road and Bye Posts.[4] Later, Wade was elected by the City Council to be one of their representatives in Parliament. He built a house close to the Abbey which was modelled on a design by Inigo Jones. It is likely that Wade, through his friendship with Allen, brought an interest in architecture to his protégé.

The development opportunities in this newly fashionable resort were initially constrained by the poor conditions of the roads leading to it. Many 17th and 18th century visitors comment on the state of the roads and some of the townspeople of Bath could understand how uneconomical it was becoming to transport goods to neighbouring towns. For more than a century, a scheme had been contemplated to make the River Avon navigable as far as the seaport of Bristol and in 1724, a stock company was formed in order to finance the venture. Ralph Allen (who became one of the three treasurers), and several members of his family, bought shares. In December 1727, the first barge moved from Bristol to Bath. Allen, with his entrepreneurial flair, probably had his eye on the new transportation system. A year earlier he had begun to acquire land at Combe Down, much of it known to bear good building stone.

Ralph Allen appears to have had many interests. During the 1720s, besides the Post Office business and the Avon navigation project, the City Council made him an "Honorary Freeman of this City' and elected him as one of the twenty Councilmen. Allen found himself in an influential position in the city. Why, then, should Ralph Allen choose to launch into another business enterprise – different from anything he had so far tried? To some extent he was at the mercy of the government, for his contract for the Cross Posts was renewable after seven years, and there were plenty of people who would have liked to see his scheme abandoned. He may have felt it wise to diversify his source of income. The first stone quarries that he bought in 1726 were on a large estate between Widcombe and Combe Down which included land belonging to the former Priory of Bath. He actively began to promote the use of his building stone outside Bath, and tendered for the contract to supply stone for part of the Greenwich hospital in London. Richard Jones suggested that the rejection of Bath stone by the architects – Campbell, James and Hawksmoor – led directly to the building of Prior Park. Allen wanted to demonstrate his faith in the beauty and quality of the stone personally and so counteract this early rejection. John Wood, the architect of so much of Bath of this period, wrote in his *Essay towards a Description of Bath* that this incident

> *brought him to a resolution to exhibit it* [i.e. the freestone] *in a Seat which he had determined to build for himself near his Works, to much greater Advantage, and in much greater Variety of Uses than it had ever appeared in any other structure.*[5]

Wood explains that Allen entered the stone business with the idea of reducing the price of the material while ensuring steady employment for the masons. Before the stone could be more widely used however, Allen had to find an efficient way of transporting the huge blocks of stone from the quarry at Combe Down to his dock on the river Avon, where they could be loaded into ships for Bristol and elsewhere. Allen commissioned a new and radical solution – the construction of an ingenious mechanical railway from the quarries at Combe Down to the Wharf already established on the Avon at Dolemead. He had probably come across such a railway before in the north of England. Wood explains that he

> then determined to make such a Road between the Summit of the Hill and the River Avon, as the Gentlemen in the North of England had made between their Collieries and the River Tyne, that heavy Carriages might be drawn along it with such little Strength, as would reduce the Transportation of the Stone to the Water Side, to half the Price of carrying it down in common Waggons.[6]

Models of railways and carriages were sent south to Bath, and Allen engaged the Bristol engineer, John Padmore, to construct the railway. The trucks were worked by horses on the level; two were used for a loaded truck, or to return an empty one uphill; loaded trucks descended the long hill by gravity. With its ingenious controls, a truck could be braked and if necessary stopped on the steepest part of the hill by one man. The cranes at Dolemead, used for loading the ships, were designed by Padmore. The commercial success of the operation was assured since the cost per ton of stone was reduced by a quarter after the railway was built.

It is possible to trace the course of the railway from the workings near de Montalt Road to the top of what is now called Ralph Allen Drive, the roadway which Allen built to accommodate the railway. It became a tourist attraction of some note in its day and was frequently commented on by visitors. An engraving by Anthony Walker of 1750, which is probably the earliest view that we have of Prior Park, gives considerable prominence to the railway and shows it surrounded by sightseers who seem more interested in the passing trucks than the fine Palladian mansion visible through the trees. The editor of the 1738 edition of Defoe's *Tour through the whole Island of Great Britain* wrote of Mr Allen

> whose Works and Inventions . . . next to the Waters, are better worth the Attention of the Curious, than anything in Bath, has a fine Wharf, and other convenient Places, to shape, to work, to imbark the Stones of many Tons Weight, which he digs from the Quarry on the adjacent Hill. This he does by a wonderful Contrivance and Machine, which runs down the Hill by Grooves plac'd in the Ground, without Horses or any other Help, than one Man to guide it, who also by a Particular Spring can stop in the steepest Part of the Hill, and in the swiftest Part of its Progress.[7]

The reference to 'grooves' was not correct; apparently this mistake was a common one, as flanged wheels, running on rails, were outside normal experience and so difficult to comprehend.

The stone wharf at Dolemead, c. 1734, by the Buck brothers

An engraving of Ralph Allen, by Henry Meyer

In 1729, Allen won the contract to supply stone to build St. Bartholomew's Hospital, London. He gradually increased his land holdings and in 1730 opened more quarries at Bathampton Down. During the 1720s, the Allens acquired a house, not far from the Abbey, with a garden, the land for which, according to Wood, was taken from the town's bowling green. Allen employed the young Wood, who was just starting on buildings for Lord Chandos (St. John's Hospital). He designed the alterations to the house in Lilliput Avenue which were required for the necessary postal services, and at the same time

> *he new fronted and raised the old Building a full Story [sic] higher; it consists of a Basement Story sustaining a double Story under the Crowning; and this is surmounted by an Attick, which created a sixth Rate House, and a Sample for the greatest Magnificence that was ever proposed by me for our City Houses.*[8]

By this time Wood was working on several projects in Bath. One of his most significant – the north side of Queen Square – was nearing completion. He had returned to Bath, from Yorkshire, inspired by the Roman and pre-Roman history of the city, and anxious to demonstrate his ideas. Already a neo-classicist, he was therefore convinced by the current mode of Palladianism. It was Wood's vision that Bath could be built

> *to vie with the famous City of Vicenza, in Italy, when in its highest Pitch of Glory, by the excellent Art of the celebrated Andrea Palladio.*[9]

Ralph Allen and John Wood began to make designs for a mansion soon after the loss of the Greenwich contract in 1728, although the serious planning, landscaping and building did not get under way until 1734. John Wood was to be able to indulge his skill and passion in designing a Palladian mansion on the hill at Combe Down which Allen now owned.

---

1. Boyce, Benjamin; *The Benevolent Man – A Life of Ralph Allen of Bath* (Harvard University Press, Cambridge, Mass., 1967).
2. The marriage took place at Charterhouse Chapel in London on 26th August 1721. Elizabeth was the daughter of Seabourne Buckeridge, a London merchant.
3. Rev. Richard Graves was Vicar of Claverton parish and a regular visitor to Prior Park in the latter years of Allen's life.
4. Richard Jones was employed by Allen as his clerk-of-works from about 1731. He wrote his autobiography around 1776 (MS in Bath Reference Library).
5. John Wood, the elder (1704-1754). His *Essay* was first published in 1742, extensively revised in 1749, and reissued in 1765. References are to the 1969 facsimile reprint of the 1765 edition, here p. 427 (Kingsmead Press, Bath, 1969).
6. Wood; op. cit., p. 424.
7. Defoe, Daniel; op. cit., p. 246.
8. Wood; op. cit., p. 245.
9. Boyce; op. cit., p. 135.

FOSSILOGICAL MAP of the Country Five Miles round BATH.

Wick Rocks
Mountain Limestone, Petrosilex &c.

Cold Aston
Great Oolite

Beach
Bas. Free Stone

Red Ground

Ring Hills
Great Oolite

Lansdown
Great Oolite

North Stoke
Bas. Free Stone

Tatwick
Bastard Free Stone

Swinford
Blue Lias

To Bristol

Lansdown
Great Oolite

Swanswick
Bas. Free Stone

Salford
Blue Lias

Shockerwick
Blue Marle

Kelweston
Blue Lias

River of Avon

Charlecombe
Bas. Free Stone

Batheaston
Calp Sand

Ashley ⊙
Great Oolite

Henley ⊙
Great Oolite

Weston
Blue Lias

To Gloucester

Lark Hall
Alluvial

To London

Coston
Coal Measures

Bathford
Bas. Free Stone

Newton
Blue Lias

White Lias
Blue Clay

Crescent Fields
Alluvial

Bath
Wick

Hampton
Bas. Free Stone

Newton Park

Alluvial

Twerton
Blue Lias

BATH

River Avon

Moukton Farley
Great Oolite

Stanton Bury
Sand under Bastard Free Stone

Inglishcomb Barrow

Warley
Bas. Free Stone

Inglishcomb
Bastard Free Stone

Farleywick
Forest Marble

Claverton Down
Great Oolite

Wilmorston
Bas. Free Stone

Prior Park
Clay under Great Oolite

Claverton
Bas. Free Stone

Combe Down
Great Oolite

Frankley
Forest Marble

South Stoke
Foot of Great Oolite

Preston
Lias

Fuller's Earth

Somerset Coal Canal

Midford
Calcan Sand

Limpley Stoke
Bas. Free Stone

Winsley
Forest Marble

To Wells

Dunkerton
Coal Measures

Combe Hay
Bastard Free Stone

Twiney
Great Oolite

Freshford
Bas. Free Stone

Roman Villa

Somerset Coal Canal

Wellow
Bastard Free Stone

Hinton
Sand

Farley Castle
Forest Marble

Ilford
Bas. Free Stone

Baggeridge
Great Oolite

Published as the Act directs by R.d Cruttwell, St James's-Street, Bath.

Gingell sculp.

2 – Like the Stages of a Roman Theatre

 The site selected for the mansion, at the head of the valley above the Lyn Brook, is without doubt one of the finest for any house, and was chosen for its own scenic quality as well as for the ready-made view. Wood described the site:

The Comb . . . extends almost to the Summit of that Hill, and terminates itself in the Shape of the Head of a vast Niche, with natural Terrasses rising above one another, like the Stages between the Seats of a Roman Theatre . . .[1]

The view from the site of the mansion was all important. The church of St. Thomas à Becket, Widcombe, and Widcombe Manor House provided the features in the landscape. Some earth-moving or levelling of the site was most likely necessary before building could commence, but essentially the form of the building that Wood designed, resulted from the existing landform and the contour pattern.

Knowledge of the underlying geology of the slope helps in understanding the scene. Bands of clay alternate with layers of limestone and it is the uneven erosion of these rocks which results in the terraced appearance. Water which drains through limestone but is forced to the surface by the clay bands, is a feature of this geology, and it causes further weathering which blurs the distinction of the different strata. Nevertheless, Wood's description of terrassing is fair; it is well illustrated in the 1785 engraving of Prior Park by Thomas Hearne, and in places it can be detected today.

It is the layers of limestone that form the potential source of building stone. The quality of the stone depends on the nature of the bedding planes. Where they are far apart, the stone can be cut freely in any direction, and is known as free-stone. Layers of limestone with bedding planes close together and containing numerous fossils are, in quarrymen's terms, ragstones or rags. The depth of the free-stone varies; on Combe Down, the stone lies some 30 feet below the surface, in beds two to four feet thick.[2] However, in some places the free-stone is much deeper than this. Combe Down stone is of sufficient

A stone quarry near Bath, drawn by J. Hassell, 1798

quality to be quarried and brought to the surface all year round. When soft, or 'green', it can be cut or sculpted very easily – one of the attributes that John Wood and Allen were quick to promote. Bath stone had been used in Roman Bath (Aquae Sulis), at least for the building of the baths, but it remained a purely local material until the 18th century, when Ralph Allen developed the quarries around Bath on a very much larger scale than previously.

There is some evidence of Roman settlements in the area. Barry Cunliffe suggests there could have been a village on Combe Down and the route to this followed the combe.[3] There was also a Roman cemetery to the south of Widcombe – perhaps in the area of Prior Park. By the 7th century, the population of the area of Lyncombe and Widcombe is said to have numbered 10 households.[4] The earthwork which crossed the fields to the south of the mansion, and is shown on many of the 19th century plans as the Wansdyke, was probably created in the 6th or 7th century.

We get a better idea of what these slopes were like in the 13th and 14th centuries from historians writing about the monks of Bath. The Widcombe land was part of the estates of the Benedictine Priory, whose monks served the cathedral church of Bath. A grange surrounded by vineyards, gardens and shady groves, stood at the foot of the valley and was used as a country residence by the Prior. The upper hillsides were used for grazing deer (for

18

The fishponds were probably enlarged to their present size when the Palladian Bridge was built

venison) and the stream was dammed to form fishponds, also a source of food; other land would have been farmed. Austin King, writing in 1895, points out that the Black Death of 1349 must have wrought severe and swift changes on the agricultural economy.[5] Wages were controlled and people could not afford to buy produce and animals, so most monasteries ceased to cultivate their farms and let them to tenants. (The difficulty with this arrangement was that there were very few tenants with sufficient money to stock their land.) King refers to an interesting lease granted by the Bath Priory, although many years after the Plague, which shows how the problem was handled. The lease is of the farm at Widcombe reserving, however, "the mansion of the Manor with court and dove houses, gardens and orchards". It includes "all that our wether flock of Combe, containing in number 340 wether sheep, and all manner of profits therefrom". The rents received comprised 16 quarters of "pure and clean and the best wheat and 22 quarters of the best barley, the cartage of certain wood, the stall feeding and fattening of one ox, and as money rent £6". The lease contains covenants to repair and cultivate, and other provisions similar to those which would be inserted in a well-drawn lease of the present day, and a special covenant to yield up at the end of the time "340 whole sound and strong sheep, not rotten, bandy, or otherwise diseased, or at the option of the Prior eighteen pence for each sheep".

19

The southern hillsides in the 1840s

Leland, in his *Itinerary* of 1535–45, visited Bath twice, before and after the Dissolution of the Monasteries in 1539.[6] On his first visit, he comments on the poor state of the wall of the parks belonging to the Bishop and Prior of Bath and observes that there are no deer.

It would seem that both the slopes and the hill tops overlooking Bath were now farmed, and there is later evidence that the hilltops were, in the 16th century, devoid of trees. Thomas Potter, writing to William Pitt in 1756, commented: "vast woods have taken possession of the naked hills",[7] and the Rev. John Collinson, in 1791, praises the large groves of fir trees planted by Ralph Allen for the "purpose of ornamenting this (at that time rough and barren hill)".[8] An engraving of as late as 1844, of the southern slopes of Bath, shows in fact only sparse tree cover (apart from the vicinity of Prior Park) and the only significant trees are hedgerow trees.

Descriptions by visitors to Prior Park later in the century, give the impression of mature trees and even of forest. A writer in the *Universal Magazine* for May 1754 lauds Allen for his sensibility to the site:

> *... he has pursued only what the natural situation has pointed out to him; and by that means rendered it one of the cheapest , and at the same time one of the most beautiful seats in England. He has levelled no hills, but enjoys the beauty of the prospects they afford; he has cut down no woods but struck through them with fine walkes ...*[9]

A survey undertaken by Thomas Thorp in 1741, of the land holdings of Ralph Allen, makes a delightful word picture as every piece of land measured is also named.[10] There are references to ownership, for example: Colethurst's Down (19 acres 1 rod 27 perches), CrossKeys Ground late Parkers (18 acres and 34 perches) and Combe Down late Mr Smith's (15 acres 1 rod and 15 perches). Could this one have been Milo Smith, the rival stone quarrier, who had been bought out by Allen? There are also names relating to the use of the field, such as Bean Close, the Rag-garden and Orchard, the Padduck [sic] and Woods, the Down above the Vineyard, all of which demonstrate a domestic scale of farming and husbandry which must have been common to all the land around a town such as Bath. In total, by 1741, Allen owned 603 acres of Widcombe and Comb (present-day Combe Down). After completing the purchase of Bathampton Manor in 1737, he had increased his holding by an additional 985 acres.

1. Wood; op.cit., p. 150.
2. Price, Liz; *Bath Freestone Workings*, p. 8 (The Resurgence Press, Radstock, 1984).
3. Cunliffe, Barry; *The City of Bath*, p. 42 (Alan Sutton, Gloucester, 1986).
4. See Aston, Mick; 'The Bath Region from Late Prehistory to the Middle Ages', pp. 73ff., in *Bath History*, vol. 1 (Alan Sutton, Gloucester, 1986), and Tyte, William; *History of Lyncombe and Widcombe*, pp. 12-13 (Bath, 1898).
5. King, Austin; *Monks of the 13th and 14th Centuries*, p. 25 (reprint, in Bath Reference Library, of a lecture given by King to the Bath Literary and Philosophical Association in 1895).
6. Leland, John; *Itinerary*, vol. 5, p. 98 (ed. Lucy Toulmin-Smith, London, 1906-10).
7. *The Correspondence of William Pitt, Earl of Chatham*, vol. 1, p. 154 (ed. Pringle and Taylor, London, 1838-40).
8. Collinson, Rev. John; *The History and Antiquities of the County of Somerset*, vol. 1, p. 150 (R. Cruttwell, Bath, 1791).
9. 'A Description of the Seat of Ralph Allen Esq. near the City of Bath', in the *Universal Magazine*, May 1754.
10. This MS survey is in Bath Reference Library.

An engraving of the North Front published in 1819

3 – A Devotion to Antiquity

 Allen's decision to build a mansion for himself was in a sense merely a symptom of the age in which he lived. The early 18th century witnessed the development of a style in English architecture – the Palladian – which popularised a set of distinct ideas as to what was good and accepted in architecture. There was, of course, a tradition of Italian Renaissance architecture in England with the work of Wren and Inigo Jones, who had introduced into design a sense of discipline. But now amongst the nobility and influential leaders of taste there was a strong feeling of kinship with the age of the Emperor Augustus. The writers of ancient Greece and Italy – Homer, Virgil, Ovid – had dominated the education of travellers on the Grand Tour in search of the pleasures of architecture and painting. The architectural designs of Palladio, publicised in a translation, by Nicolas Dubois, of *I quattro libri dell'architettura*, illustrated the spirit of the new feeling, as did another publication, of 1715 – *Vitruvius Britannicus* by Colen Campbell.

The Palladian taste was also closely allied to that of the second generation whig aristocracy. Palladianism in England was more than a question of aesthetics; it was held to demonstrate restraint and moderation, and was also a reflection of the political views of the time. Although the mid 18th century was to become the age of the country house, no-one wished to look extravagant. (By contrast, Blenheim Palace by Vanburgh was held in poor esteem by the Palladians – it violated the canons of Taste which the aristocracy, in particular Lord Burlington and his friends, had established.) A further fascination of Palladio's work was the interest in and exploitation of harmonic proportions. In architectural circles, arguments polarised between those who believed that the architecture of antiquity embraced a complete rational system of architecture and those who held that innovation was permissible. Sir John Summerson has aptly summarised this, noting that the dawning philosophy of Whiggism was ready to accept a thesis which took in "at one and the same time, a devotion to antiquity, a flexibility authorised jointly by Palladio and common sense, and a strong national loyalty in the figure of Inigo Jones".[1]

John Wood, a native of Bath, whose father George worked as a builder in the city, was twenty-three when he started work seriously in Bath. He returned

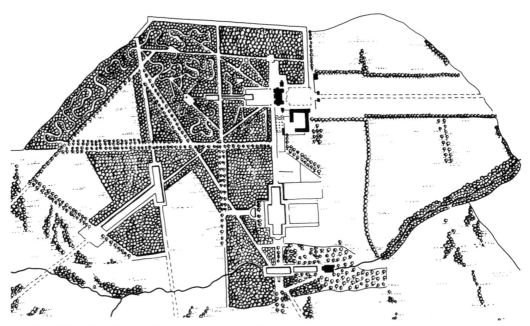

Part of John Wood's plan of Bramham Park, a combination of water features, winding walks and long vistas

to take up the development possibilities offered by this expanding city, intent on improving its architectural style. Wood's ideas of improvement were influenced by Palladio, and it was not surprising that Ralph Allen should use him as his architect in his buildings of Bath.

For Wood, there were probably two other external factors which influenced his designs in Bath, besides the Palladian movement. The first was his employment as a young man by Robert Benson, Lord Bingley, at his seat in Yorkshire, Bramham Park, and the experience he gained there probably contributed to his ideas on siting the mansion at Prior Park. Lord Bingley probably purchased his estate in 1699; it is likely that planting here started almost as soon as the siting of the house had been fixed. During his employment of 1724–25, Wood made designs for an aqueduct, possibly designed the central section of the stables, and prepared a plan of the layout of the garden. Wood's plan shows the slopes that enclose the parterre behind the house to have been densely planted and to have winding walks running through the forest and continuing beyond. Arthur Oswald suggests that this must have been among the earliest instances of naturalism brought close to a house, being not much later than the wilderness of Hampton Court.[2] However, there is some speculation as to the identity of Bramham's landscape designer. Charles Bridgeman was the first to design in this style but little is known of his activities before 1709. Alternatively, Stephen Switzer is a possibility. He was an acknowledged expert on the use of water, which was an important element of the Bramham landscape. He also had a practice in the north of England and was an early advocate of naturalism.

The water features at Bramham were significant, and in Wood's day it would have been these features which contrasted with the ranks of beech trees

24

through which the rides were cut. Ornaments and garden buildings were added after Wood left and as the century progressed.

The position chosen for the house at Bramham was high up a long slope on the west side of a valley with a wide view across it north–eastwards. The front of the house faces east-north-east. It is approached from the north by a Roman road, and the view from the approach road was of the house "backed by the serried beeches of the garden on the still higher ground behind".[3] Benson had received a sound classical education and visited Italy. He was probably his own architect to the extent of the siting and general character of the house, but it is considered likely that Thomas Archer was involved for the details. The interior of the house is described by a visitor in 1717: she found that "the hall is remarkable, all finished within with stone and the pillars in it finely carved", a feature which Wood specified later for Prior Park, although he was probably guided by Ralph Allen's wishes.[4]

It is interesting to note that at Bramham House the garden layout was conceived as an equivalent to the house if not of greater importance, entitled to its own orientation, and not ancillary to the mansion. Christopher Hussey has pointed out that this thinking led "to the mansion becoming an incident, albeit an important one in wholly decentralised landscape scenery".[5]

The second strong influence on Wood was the work of Colen Campbell which, more especially, would have been of significance to an equally well-informed Allen. The country house boom of the 1720s and 1730s provided the impetus necessary to demonstrate the Palladian style, already aided by *Vitruvius Britannicus*, and came just at the right moment it seems, when the whig owners' wish to replace their Tudor and Stuart manor-houses with something more modern was at its strongest. Much space in *Vitruvius Britannicus* is given to existing architects' work, among them Vanburgh, Hawksmoor, Archer, etc. However, Campbell includes his own design for Wanstead in Essex and manages, according to Summerson, to use this work to display himself as the author of the purest, largest and most classical house of the day. There were three designs for Wanstead and all were to prove classic statements by which English country house designs were influenced, directly or indirectly, for half a century. The Wanstead designs were made around 1717, but it was not until 1733 that three other houses were begun which were conscious derivations of Campbell's work: two in Yorkshire – Wentworth Woodhouse, built by Henry Flitcroft, and Nostell Priory by Sir Rowland Winn; and, of course, Prior Park. These three designs, all derived from Palladio, took the form of a main house with two winged blocks, with the central mansion close to Campbell's Wanstead model.

Wood implies that it was the elevations of Prior Park that were closely copied from Wanstead. He described the Prior Park mansion thus:

For the Sake of Novelty, the Outside of the Building shews in its Rear an Hexastyle Frontispiece composed of Ionick Columns supporting a Corinthian Entablature, divested of its Beauty for the Convenience of such Windows as

25

Elevations of the original design for Wanstead (above) and Prior Park (below). Wood's plans show rectangular broken staircases descending from the Portico, but these were never built

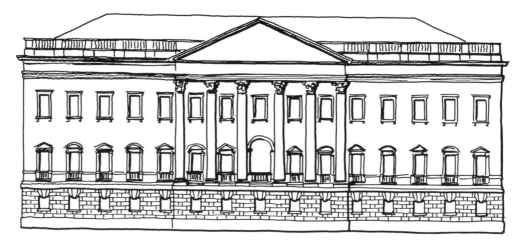

would give a Prospect to the Garrets; but in the Front the Architecture is more compleat; and Mr. Colen Campbell having boasted of the Justness of the Hexastyle Porticoe Designed by him before Wansted House [sic] in Essex, it was determined that a juster Hexastyle Porticoe should be executed before this House, and with Columns of a larger Size; and for this End I Designed it with Columns of three Feet one Inch and a half Diameter, which exceeds those at Wansted by an Inch and a half; made the Intercolumnations of that Kind which Vitruvius calls Systylos; and gave two compleat Intercolumnations to the Flank of our Porticoe, instead of the compleat Interval and small Portion of another at Wansted.[6]

Ralph Allen himself, it is said, insisted on the sturdier columns. As at Wentworth Woodhouse, the wings were designed to consist of two pedimented service blocks and two towers; but the whole composition was bent round the sides of an elongated dodecagon – a form suggested by the contours of the combe in which the house is built. At Prior Park the siting of the house and its relationship to its landscape is of particular significance. Whereas at other Palladian-style mansions the landscape is rarely referred to, at Prior Park it is an integral part of the design and layout. The grounds of Wanstead are mentioned by many historians as being attractive to visitors, although George Robertson's engraving of Wanstead House shows a walled parterre in front of the house, a feature which was common for the period.[7] There were a number of theories of gardening published in the early 18th century – among them John James' *Theory and Practice of Gardening* (published in 1712); d'Argenville (1709); and Philip Miller (1724). Most of these authors tended to extol the virtues of the French school of gardening, where stress was laid on the parterre "which should be next to the house", and the use of woodland groves. The 'natural' sinuous lines of garden design, which were to become the fashion amongst the smart set, were overlooked. Very often a designed landscape was not in immediate juxtaposition to the buildings; even at Bramham the house relates only to the small parterre; and at Rousham (1725), Claremont (1716) and Stourhead (first designed in 1721 by Colen Campbell), nowhere is the landscape garden close to the house. At Prior Park the view from the house, almost by chance, provides the classic picturesque scene, now so highly valued.

Wood, with his passion for antiquity in general and Rome in particular, is likely to have read Pope's essay in *The Guardian* (of 1713) which deduced from Homer and Virgil that "the Taste of the Ancients in their Gardens" was for "the amiable Simplicity of unadorned Nature".[8] Robert Castell's *Villas of the Ancients* corroborated this viewpoint and Charles Bridgeman, main protagonist at the time, is suggested by Hussey to have been the perfect landscape designer for the Palladian house.[9] Wood, however, does not go into detail on landscape, although he does relate his buildings at Prior Park to a "bason" of water lower down the valley. Wood's General Plan for Prior Park is lettered according to the Diagram. The first part to be built was the Westward Wing of Offices (E); then the Square Pavilion (C) was erected; after that the Mansion House (A)

The General Plan of Mr. Allen's House and Offices as first designed by John Wood

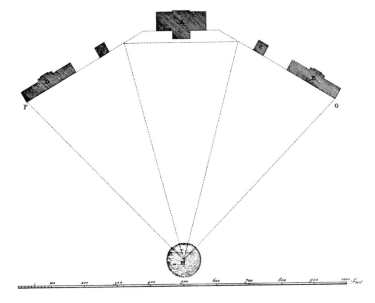

was begun and "in the next place, the three Piles of Building were United before the Foundations were Laid for any of the remaining Parts of the Seat". The western wing housed Stables and Coach Houses with a Harness Room, a Barn and Granaries, a Hay House and Pigeon Loft. Wood explains that the Stables were designed to be arched in stone,

> Mr. Hanbury's Stables at Ponty Pool in Monmouthshire, which I went purposely to see, furnishing us with the Example.[10]

The roof treatment was altered from the original drawing, as Ralph Allen wished to use stone for the roof. The Stables were lined throughout with wrought free-stone. Wood, writing some years after completion of this wing, was able to comment on this difference which occurred from the plan and elevations.

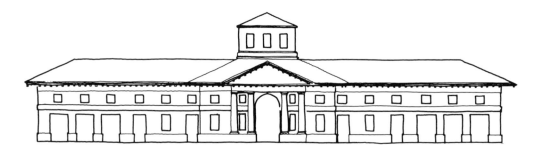

The design for the western wing (the stable block) from Wood's Essay on Bath. Compare this elevation with the print by Walker of 1754.

The Pavilion was built partly "for Coaches to stop under, and partly for Pigeons to reside in". This whole unit is built from wrought free-stone and Wood comments:

> . . . the Pigeons are magnificently Housed . . . So that if a Beautiful Habitation is really an Allurement to this Species of Birds, as some pretend, Mr Allen's Pigeons will, in all Probability, never desert their present Place of Abode.[11]

The colonnades between the Pavilion and the mansion housed the "tamer Poultry"; the Allens were known to keep guinea fowl and chickens. The accommodation consisted of "three Rooms Fronting Southward, with three Apertures, Arched over, to every room; and the Whole is built with wrought Free Stone. . ." It was apparently necessary to build the Pavilion at some two feet, six inches lower than was originally intended so that the "Beauty proposed by a Continuation of the Basement Lines of every Part of the Seat, was inevitably lost".[12]

The basement plan of the mansion shows two flights of steps descending from the Portico above, very similar to the Wanstead elevations, but clearly another part of the design which was never built. The western wing was completed around 1737 and the mansion started soon after. Wood does not comment on the "bason" of water (marked H); how successful it might have been and whether it was ever placed there is not known. Not shown on early plans of Prior Park are the Porters' Lodges at the top and bottom of the carriage drive, also designed by Wood. The roofing material here was also stone, laid in projecting courses, but now altered.[13] The carriage drive, being private, was gated, and these delightful gate-keepers' cottages served to introduce and protect the estate. The buildings described above were completed under Wood's superintendence by 1748.

Soon after this, Wood's temper provoked a disagreement with Ralph Allen over some details of decoration, and Wood left his employment. The argument was clearly not of lasting consequence as he writes equably of Allen in the second edition of his *Essay*. Nevertheless, this cessation of Wood's employment meant that Allen's clerk of works, Richard Jones, was put in charge of the eastern range of buildings and, whereas symmetry was the intention of Wood in his overall design, Jones changed the layout and ruined this balance. However, the landscape setting and the spectacular view were not compromised in any way and, in 1742, Wood was able to boast that from the Pavilion, or Portico, "there is a Prospect as Beautiful as a compact City at the Bottom of a Rich Vale, surrounded with Fertile Hills can possibly furnish the Eye with".[14]

1. Summerson, Sir John; *Architecture in Britain, 1530-1830*, p. 321 (Penguin Books, Harmondsworth, 1953).
2. Oswald, Arthur; 'A Yorkshire Landscape Garden' in *Country Life*, June 1958, pp. 1294-96. This article was part of a series on Bramham Park over several months in 1958.
3. Oswald; op.cit. p. 1295.
4. Hussey, Christopher; *English Gardens and Landscapes 1700-1750*, p. 74 (Country Life, London, 1967).
5. Hussey; op.cit., p. 74.
6. Wood; op.cit., p. 432.
7. Published in Summerson; op.cit., p. 323.
8. An extract is quoted in Hunt, J. Dixon and Willis, P.; *The Genius of the Place – The English Landscape Garden 1620-1820*, p. 205 (Paul Elek, London, 1975).
9. A facsimile edition was published by Garland Publishing, London, 1982, edited by J. Dixon Hunt.
10. Wood; op.cit., p. 427.
11. Wood; op.cit., p. 429.
12. Wood; op.cit., p. 429.
13. Early photographs show the Middle Lodge with a stone roof.
14. Wood; op.cit., p. 431.

Thy Taste refin'd appears in yonder Wood,

Not *Nature* tortur'd, but by *Art* improv'd;

Where *cover'd Walks* with *open Vistas* meet,

An *Area* here, and there a *shady Seat*.

A thousand Sweets in mingled Odours flow

From blooming *Flow'rs*, which on the Borders grow.

In num'rous Streams the murm'ring Waters thrill,

Uniting all, obedient to thy Will;

Till, by thy Art, in *one Canal* combin'd,

They thro' the *Wood* in various *Mazes* wind;

From thence the foaming Waves fall rapid down,

In bold *Cascades*, and lash the rugged Stone.

But here their Fury lost, the calmer Scene

Delights the softer Muse, and Soul serene:

An ample *Bason*, Centre of the Place,

In Lymph transparent holds the scaly Race;

Its glassy Face, from ev'ry Ruffle free,

Reflects the Image of each neighb'ring Tree;

On which the *feather'd Choir* melodious throng,

By Love inspir'd, unite in tuneful Song;

Part of Mary Chandler's poem, A Description of Bath, where she describes the future ambience of Prior Park

4 – A Pretty Landskip

 At the same time as these changes were emerging in architectural style – derived largely from classical antiquity and the popular reverence for Palladianism – similar opinions and changes were being wrought in the way in which landscape and gardens were considered. There were a number of features to these changes, not all due to differences in artistic taste. The Versailles pattern of landscape – of elaborate waterworks, embroidery-style flowerbeds and complicated parterres or Knotgardens, adopted by the country estate owners of 17th century Britain – was found to be very expensive to maintain, needing a large workforce of gardeners to keep it looking as it should. The many acres of forest planting, vistas and long avenues took up large amounts of otherwise profitable agricultural land, and the whole idea was very often beyond the means of the average land-owner. Furthermore, this ostentatious display of the use of land was not necessarily appropriate to the more democratic political climate of the early 18th century.

There were also other factors to consider. The young nobility taking a Grand Tour, brought back to England ideas and visions of dramatic landscapes of the Alps and the Apennines, as well as the discovery of the literature of antiquity. It was the way in which these writers glorified the peace of rural life, and the love they demonstrated of natural beauty that was to impress and inspire, and profoundly to influence garden design in 18th century England.

It was no accident that the developments of literature and painting went hand-in-hand with the similar thoughts on landscape of the early 18th century. The interplay between the three disciplines was the essence, the spirit of the age. Walpole was to write much later in the century: "Poetry, Painting and Gardening, or the science of Landscape, will forever by men of Taste be deemed Three Sisters, or the Three New Graces who dress and adorn Nature".[1] The important starting point for what we now know as the English Landscape Movement was an acceptance and a respect for Nature as opposed to Art. The moral significance of beauty – linked strongly with a respect for nature – became an issue. In 1709, the third Earl of Shaftesbury wrote of these morals drawn from scenery:

Your Genius, the Genius of the Place, and the GREAT GENIUS have at last prevail'd. I shall no longer resist the Passion growing in me for Things of a natural kind; where neither Art, nor the Conceit or Caprice of Man has spoil'd their genuine Order, by breaking in upon that primitive state. Even the rude Rocks, the mossy Caverns, the irregular unwrought Grotto's, and broken Falls of Waters, with all the horrid Graces of the Wilderness itself, as representing NATURE more, will be the more engaging, and appear with a Magnificence beyond the formal Mockery of Princely Gardens.[2]

Joseph Addison, in *The Spectator* in 1712, writes in more practical vein of the advantages of the Works of Nature compared with the "very defective" works of Art and of the feelings of Passions associated with scenery:

. . . there is generally in Nature something more Grand and August, than what we meet with in the Curiosities of Art. When, therefore, we see this imitated in any measure, it gives us a nobler and more exalted kind of Pleasure than what we receive from the nicer and more accurate Productions of Art.

He goes on to describe the pleasures derived from natural scenery:

But why may not a whole Estate be thrown into a kind of Garden by frequent Plantations, that may turn as much to the Profit, as the Pleasure of the Owner? A Marsh overgrown with Willows, or a Mountain shaded with Oaks, are not only more beautiful, but more beneficial, than when they lie bare and unadorned. Fields of Corn make a pleasant Prospect, and if the Walks were a little taken care of that lie between them, if the natural Embroidery of the Meadows were helpt and improved by some small Additions of Art, and the several Rows of Hedges set off by Trees and Flowers, that the Soil was capable of receiving, a Man might make a pretty Landskip of his own Possessions.[3]

Addison wrote a number of essays on the landscape garden, and was one of its foremost promoters. Many of the contemporary writers commenting on gardens and landscapes were either landowners like Lord Burlington, travellers like Defoe and Evelyn, or writers and poets like Jame Thomson and Alexander Pope.

Pope, who was to be so influential at Prior Park, did not write professionally as a gardener and, compared with some writers such as William Shenstone and Horace Walpole, he contributed little directly to gardening literature. He was one of the coterie surrounding Lord Burlington and during his life took great interest in what Burlington was designing and initiating at Chiswick. More importantly, he was also a practical gardener himself, and his own small garden at Twickenham was justly famous during his lifetime. He published few essays on gardening and we learn of most of his ideas from his private correspondence with friends whom he helped and advised on their garden projects. His first essay on gardening fashions – in *The Guardian* of 1713 – illustrates Pope's grounding in classical antiquity. He had made extensive

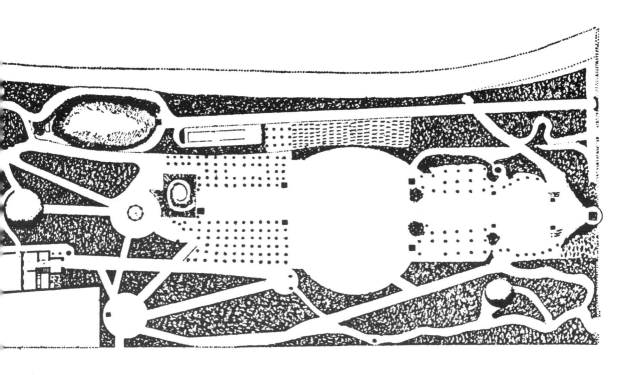

The Plan of Pope's Twickenham garden, begun in 1720 and drawn by John Serle. The garden was roughly 200 yds by 100 yds, about 4 acres. It was approached by way of the grotto, the underground passage beneath the house, and included a small vineyard and pineapple stores.

translations of many of the classical writers such as Homer, Virgil and Martial, and had absorbed the ideas of rural retirement that these writers encouraged. He also captured the essential elements of gardening, as recorded by Joseph Spence in his *Anecdotes*, that "all gardening is landscape-painting", demonstrating too that he was familiar with the works of the fashionable French artists, Claude le Lorrain and Poussin.[4] Pope's later writing evokes similar scenes to those depicted in the landscapes of Claude.

Pope was also known to have read Pliny's letters describing his famous villas at Tusculum and Laurentum. They were publicised by Robert Castell's translation and commentary, which had been published with Lord Burlington's sponsorship. The word 'villa' in the Roman sense included not just the house and garden but the estate as well, and these letters provided the most informative surviving accounts of Roman garden design. What is interesting is the spacious layout of these houses and their relationship with the garden and landscape, which makes it difficult sometimes to determine where the house finishes and the garden begins. On reading the letters, it is striking to note the variety of landscape and its constituent planting. In one corner of the estate at Tusculum, for example, *when you are arrived at the end of all these winding alleys, you come out into a strait walk; nay, not into one, but into several; divided, in some places, by grass-plots, in others, by box-trees, cut into a thousand shapes . . . and now and then, in the midst of a plot, improved with all imaginable art, you meet, on a sudden, with a spot of ground, wild and uncultivated, as if transplanted hither on purpose.*[5]

Castell's commentary picks up the happy juxtaposition of the two sorts of garden styles – the "Ground and Plantations" laid out "by the Rule and Line", and the parts of the estate which imitated the country, and where nature was allowed to flourish.[6]

Pope must also have been well-read in 17th century, as well as contemporary, writers on gardens and landscape. His *Guardian* essay is based around his translation of Homer's account of Alcinous' gardens, but Peter Martin suggests that his accompanying commentary may be traced directly to Sir William Temple and his long meditation *Upon the Gardens of Epicurus* (first published in 1692).[7] Temple also bases his essay on classical sources but he is especially interesting for being the first to discuss the Chinese style of planting in which

their greatest Reach of Imagination is employed in contriving Figures, where the Beauty shall be great, and strike the Eye, but without any Order or Disposition of Parts, that shall be commonly or easily observ'd.[8]

Temple goes on to warn of the difficulties inherent in achieving this concept of irregularity. The other writer on which Pope relied heavily for his *Guardian* article was Joseph Addison;[9] indeed, Pope takes up many of the themes of both writers without very much development of them, although the essay did serve to indicate more than a passing interest in garden design. But it was not until 1731, when he wrote *A Master Key to Popery or a True and Perfect Key to Pope's Epistle to the Earl of Burlington*, that he declares his agreement with the current principles of design.[10] From 1719, when he moved into his Palladian villa by the river at Twickenham, he was busy planning and planting his own garden, exploring pictorial effects and demonstrating his three principles of gardens which he later confided to Spence as being "the contrasts, the management of surprises, and the concealment of the bounds".[11] The garden has gone now, but a plan by John Serle remains, which shows the clear influence of the French style, although we should remember that in the 1720s, any garden that was not of the parterre and symmetrical avenues pattern, would have seemed natural and original. The Twickenham garden has to be seen as part of the continuum in taste that leads on eventually to the naturalism of Brown and Repton.

Pope had a number of friends, all in the Burlington set, who were also at that time planning landscapes of their own and, just as later he was to visit Prior Park, so he often went to see his acquaintants at such places as Cirencester, Sherborne, Rousham and Stowe. He became deeply involved in Lord

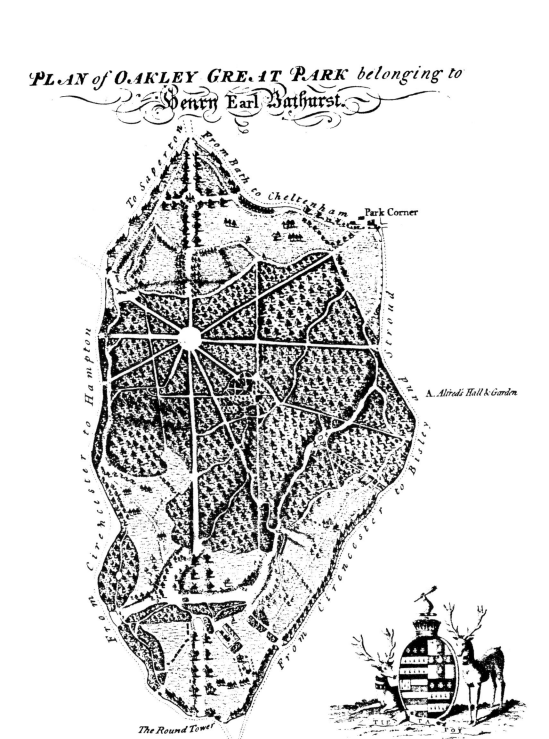

PLAN of OAKLEY GREAT PARK belonging to Henry Earl Bathurst.

To Saperton

From Bath to Cheltenham

Park Corner

To Saperton

Cirencester to Hampton

Stroud

A. Alfred's Hall & Garden

From Cirencester to Bisley

From Cirencester to Bisley

The Round Tower

Bathurst's planting schemes for Cirencester Park, where Bathurst favoured a grand style more in common with Fontainebleau and Compiègne – the "vast vistas . . . aligned on distant landmarks or linking with *rond-points*".[12] Pope also

35

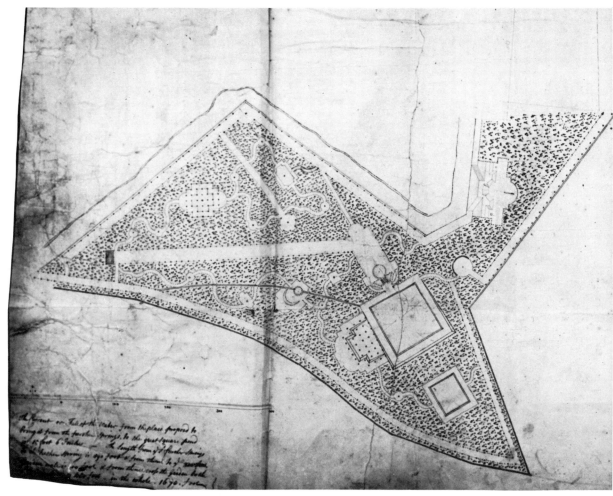

The plan of Rousham attributed to Chrles Bridgeman, c. 1725 at the time when Pope first visited it

contributed to Lord Digby's garden at Sherborne Castle, where he was fascinated by the nature of the site. In his letters he writes of the "solemnity" and "prodigious beauty" of the valley of the River Yeo. Here for the first time in his gardening experience, he was to comprehend, as Martin says, "the philosophical and imaginative uses within a garden of . . . thick woods, the sound and sight of water, rustic stonework of grottoes and old seats and bridges".[13] Another garden that he came to know well was at Rousham, designed in the 1720s by Charles Bridgeman, for whose work he was enthusiastic. It was the water features that Pope seemed to like most. Writing to Martha Blount he describes the pleasure garden of Rousham as "the prettiest place for water-falls, jetts, ponds inclosed with beautiful scenes of green and hanging wood".[14]

However, it was Stowe that seems to have made the most lasting impression, giving him and other visitors the most satisfaction. He first saw the gardens in 1724 as they were originally laid out by Bridgeman. It is accepted now that

36

in the 1730s, he also took great interest and helped in the treatment given to William Kent's Elysian Fields at Stowe. This was an area more romantically pretty than the earlier parts of the garden, and contained the features that Pope was advocating in a landscape: a grotto, a serpentine, a little valley into which water flowed from the grotto, and steep grassy banks, with thin screens of trees which were characteristic of Kent's effort to create a sequence of pictures.[15] His main contribution to all these gardens in the first 40 years of the 18th century was his encouragement and artistic support of the owners of the landscapes, and this is no less true of Ralph Allen and his landscape at Prior Park. Later, we shall see how far he helped Allen.

Pope spent his life writing poetry, and writing to and visiting his many friends, often undertaking long and arduous journeys. Ralph Allen and his wife, on the other hand, were fairly settled in Bath. Although Allen had travelled extensively in connection with setting up the postal business, his council work and his quarrying business probably kept him tied to the city. In 1735, the Allens, perhaps impatient to move up to their planned mansion at Combe Down and perhaps tiring of the noise and hassle of living in Lilliput Avenue surrounded by the postal business, decided to move to a house across the river in Widcombe. There is little information as to exactly where this house might have been. An engraving of 1737 by Pinchbeck, from a drawing by Speren, is said to be of this house. It is shown adjoining the stone-waggon track, but on the 1742 Thorp plan, it is difficult to find a house or building of any kind which is both in Widcombe and close to the track.

Allen's first wife died early in 1736, and he married Elisabeth Holder in March 1737. Allen himself was now becoming something of a personality in the city. His portrait was painted for the Council room, and his plans for building the mansion at Prior Park were the news of the day.

In 1734, Pope was in Bath – he had often visited the Spa along with Lord Burlington, Lord Bolingbroke, and George Lyttleton. This was the same year that Princess Amelia (daughter to George II) visited the city and the local poetess Mary Chandler dedicated her poem *The Description of Bath* to the Princess.[16] *The Description* introduces the history of Bath and contains something on the medicinal quality of the waters, a social survey and a panoramic survey of the town, river and surrounding hills. It ends with lines on Ralph Allen. She is considerably guided by the thinking of the day on gardens and landscaping in her description of Allen's proposals for the grounds of Prior Park. To some extent she writes of what it could be expected that the contemporary fashionable country house and its park would or should contain. Architecture and gardening were becoming the polite accomplishments of every gentleman and woman and the attributes of a typical landscape of the 1730s would have been well known. As a poetess she had probably also read Pope (his *Epistle to Burlington* was written in 1731) and she may have met him in Bath. Having said this much, the poem was still remarkable and was indeed "Prophetic", turning out, as we shall see, to be very close to reality.

*The house at Widcombe thought to be the
home of the Allens from 1735 to 1737*

No doubt, being a Bathonian, Chandler knew the nature of the site well, but it is interesting to see that she pays some attention to the many springs on the land which could be channelled into one, so that

> *From thence the foaming Waves fall rapid down,*
> *In bold Cascades, and lash the rugged Stone.*

We shall see in a later chapter how this particular factor became a significant feature in the design. She also mentions woodland in terms of existing maturity. Indeed, some trees may need to be felled to transform the woodland

> *Where cover'd Walks with open Vistas meet,*
> *An Area here, and there a shady Seat.*

The poem's publication must have thrown Ralph Allen even more into the limelight in Bath, and even if Alexander Pope had not heard of the plans for the Widcombe hillside at that time, this poem must have aroused his interest. Here were the principles to which Pope subscribed, being publicly advocated for one of the local estates. In fact, Pope had probably heard of Allen by now from Lord Burlington, who had acquired stone from Allen's quarries some six years before. However, Allen probably may not have known a great deal about Pope, that is until he read a pirated 1735 edition of his letters. This edition puts the poet in a good light as an approachable, amenable and knowledgeable person, knowledgeable particularly regarding gardens and the treatment of landscape, but it was not the complete correspondence, and Ralph Allen's response on reading it was to write to Pope to offer to sponsor a new and complete edition of the poet's letters.[17] Those that he had read so far had convinced Allen that here was someone who was an expert on the new forms of landscaping. With the plans for the Widcombe estate just coming together, some friendly advice could be useful.

1. Quoted in Hunt and Willis; op.cit., p.11.
2. Quoted in Hunt and Willis; op.cit., p. 124. The quotation is from 'The Moralists – A Rhapsody', published in *Characteristics of Men, Manners, Opinions* (Times, 1711).
3. Quoted in Hunt and Willis, op.cit., p. 142.
4. Spence, Joseph; *Observations, Anecdotes and Characters of Men*, p. 252 (ed. Osborn, J., Oxford University Press, 1966).
5. *Letters of Pliny the Younger* (trans. Earl of Orrery, London, 1751).
6. Castell; op.cit., quoted in Hunt and Willis; op.cit., p. 187.
7. Martin, Peter; *Pursuing Innocent Pleasures – The Gardening World of Alexander Pope*, p. 5 (Archon Books, Hamden, Connecticut, 1984).
8. Quoted in Hunt and Willis, op.cit., p. 99.
9. Suggested by Martin; op.cit., p. 7.
10. An extract is quoted in Hunt and Willis; op.cit., p. 211.
11. Spence; op.cit., p. 254.
12. Hussey; op.cit., p. 80.
13. Martin; op.cit., p. 15.
14. *Correspondence of Alexander Pope*, vol. 2, p. 513 (ed. Sherburn, G., Oxford University Press, 1956).
15. These features are listed by Martin; op.cit., p. 14.
16. Chandler, Mary; *A Description of Bath, A Poem* (Bath 1734).
17. *Mr. Pope's Literary Correspondence for Thirty Years from 1704-1735, Being a Collection of Letters, which passed between him and Several Eminent Persons* (Edmund Curll, 1735).

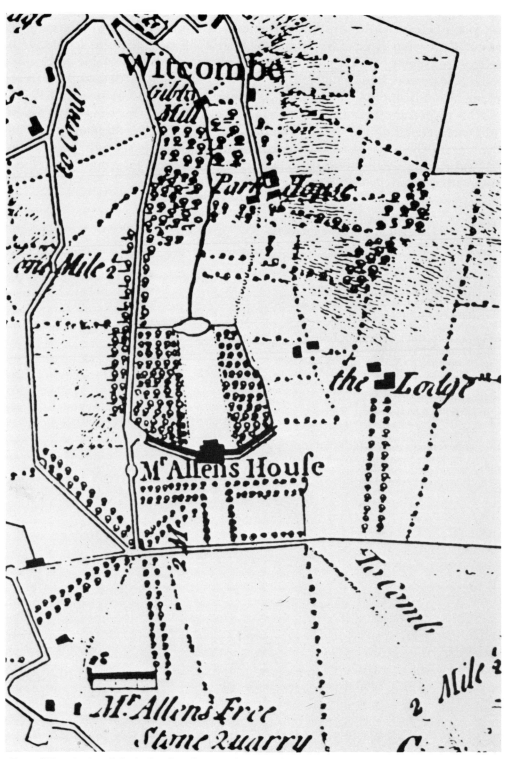

Part of Thorp's map of 1742 of Bath and Five Miles around

5 – Mr. Allen's Gardens

 We have already speculated as to the state of the landscape where Allen decided to build his mansion in Widcombe. Clearly Allen was well aware of the fashions of the day and was not the only person with resources to wish for a Palladian mansion and a fine park. He was well acquainted, he had the services of an excellent gardener, Isaac Dodsley, and he now had that doyen of the new style of English landscaping and gardening, Alexander Pope, to advise him. John Wood was also familiar with garden designs and was still working for him.

Not long after Allen's offer to Pope to finance the new edition of his letters, came the first visit to the poet, and at the beginning of April 1736, Allen saw the famous Twickenham garden, grotto and house. Having already supplied Lord Burlington with stone, Allen was also able to visit Chiswick to see the gardens there and the use to which his stone had been put. These two places showed what could be done in a small space together with the imaginative use of water and plantations in the landscape. This was good timing, coinciding as it did with the start of building operations and the landscape planning of the Prior Park mansion.

In September 1737, Pope in turn came to see Prior Park for the first time. He could only stay for a few days as it was a flying visit from Cirencester where he was helping Lord Bathurst. Pope was in the habit of visiting his friends for long periods at a time – generally their estates were in need of friendly advice as well. At the same time he took his own garden at Twickenham seriously, ordering (in 1738) stone urns from Allen, to his own design, and borrowing Allen's mason, William Biggs, to set up these urns. Pope helped to sell Allen's stone to some of these other country house owners; for example, he spent some time arranging for Allen to send a 'Pillar' to Sir Thomas Lyttleton at Hagley.

In November 1739, Pope finally arrived at the Allen household for a three month visit. From correspondence with friends, Pope's intention was to "read, and plant away my time, leaving the Madness of the Little Town [Bath] beneath me".[1]

From a letter written to Allen in May 1740, three months after this visit, it would seem that the gardens were almost finished. His letter hints at the "large amount of planting cutting of paths through woods, clearing of prospects, management of water and so on" that must have gone on during the winter. Pope looks forward to seeing the gardens finished and enquired after the state of the "Elms we planted on each Side of the Lawn and of the Little Wood-work to join one wood to the other below, which I hope you planted this Spring".[2]

Thorp's map of 1742, entitled *Survey of Five Miles round Bath*, is one of the earliest maps of the Bath area which includes Prior Park. This shows the Prior Park landscape following the pattern set out by Wood, of the mansion overlooking an open area, probably lawn-lined on either side, with substantial plantations leading down to a water-filled "bason". Peter Martin suggests that the "little wood-work" joining upper and lower woods could be the thin line of trees along the western side of the lawn below the "bason" and that this could well have been Pope's idea since he asked about it in particular.[3] It would have been characteristic of the poet; it provides not only visual continuity and concealment of the bounds, but also a line of woods through which a path could be cut. A path still runs along the western boundary wall, constructed on a terrace, and is still clearly defined.

To the south of the mansion, the map shows the avenues of trees which focus on the south entrance to the mansion, and the avenues centering on what is now the Upper Lodge, the junction of Ralph Allen Drive and Claverton Down Road. The *patte d'oie* figure, which results from planting in converging avenues, was probably no accident but a feature of the forest style of planting which can be seen at places like Cirencester and Bramham Park. Richard Jones later recorded that 55,146 trees, mainly pines, were planted all around the estate, and no doubt these trees were some of that number. Jones also says that in 1742

> he [Allen] *began to plant the warren, which was a rabbit warren before. The first portion planted is now called Fir Forest, and then he began to plant firs all over his estate, which extended five miles in length: his coach roads through his estate measured at least ten miles.*[4]

Some of the street names of Combe Down today bear witness to the trees that once stood there.

More than elm and Scots pine were planted. In the gardens above Middle Gate (the main entrance now), a mixture of oak and beech together with larch, bay, laurels, yew, holly, cedar and Spanish chestnut are recorded in the Estate Accounts made after Allen's death.

On the terrace to the south of the mansion, a memorial statue was placed to honour Allen's friend and patron, General George Wade. Before he died in 1748 Wade had been granted the titles of Field Marshal and Commander-in-Chief of the British forces in Flanders and then in England. The memorial represented him in Roman dress, and around the base were stone panels depicting in high relief the works that Wade had carried out in Scotland. Although the statue has not survived, three of the panels remain and are

42

displayed inside the mansion. The land above the statue was still in use as a deer park at this time, deer having probably been reintroduced in the early 1740s.

In fact, deer were grazing this land at least until the 1760s. Pope, writing to Allen, has some advice on the management of Fawns.[5] There is a record of 16 Headed Deer, 26 Does, one Gelt Deer, 11 Fawns and 5 Prucketts which were sold to Mrs Allen for £32.6s.8d. in 1764. There is no mention of deer in the park after this date and I suspect that when Allen's successors at Prior Park, the Warburtons, left, they sold all of the remainder.

The other main building shown on the 1742 map is the Lodge, a Gothic style cottage built in 1740 by Richard Jones for Allen's gardener, Dodsley. Peach, writing in 1895, called it "a small, but very pretty cottage".[6] Other 18th century maps show the cottage in the midst of fields, and the 1742 map indicates an avenue of trees stretching southwards. The Gothic style was to become of some significance later in the century, but at 1740 this must be one of the earliest examples of a revival in the Gothic taste. The building originally had a hipped roof as shown in the margin of the plan prepared around 1758 by Thomas Thorp and John Overton, and legend has it that the cottage includes stones from the medieval Priory buildings at the foot of the hill.

The Lodge or Gardener's House, now extended. The Porch was originally on this elevation

The early 18th century was a time when the garden grotto was at its most fashionable. Either a naturally occurring cave or something specially constructed, it gave an opportunity to display and enjoy the rocks, fossils and shells collected avidly by its owners.

Shells were the most commonly used material to start with, but later "specimens of minerals, felspar and fossils joined the shells, and the lovely glittering collections, fresh from the sea ... were turned into grottoes".[7] They were probably highly impracticable even as garden buildings, and they must have cost much in time and money but Barbara Jones observes: "nothing in all architecture can have been more beautiful than one of the great grottoes in its heyday".[8] Pope was no exception to this enthusiasm and he readily helped a number of friends, among them Mrs Howard at Marble Hill, whom he supplied with shells and Cornish minerals that he was receiving from William Borlase; and Mrs Mary Caesar at Bennington Hall in the 1720s. His own grotto at Twickenham must have been astounding if the description by his gardener, John Serle, is anything to go by. The source of some of these rocks was quite remarkable in itself. Serle describes some of the contents:

> *Several pieces of Crystal with a brown Incrustation and a Mixture of Mundic from the Hartz Mines in Germany; a fine Piece of Gold Ore from the Peruvian Mines; Silver Ore from the Mines of Mexico; several Pieces of Silver Ore from Old Spain; some large Pieces of Gold Clift from Mr Cambridge, in Gloucestershire; Lead Ore, Copper Ore, white Spar, petrified Wood, Brazil Pebbles, Egyptian Pebbles and Blood-stones from Mr Brinsden. Some large Clumps of Amethyst, and several Pieces of White Spar, from the Duchess of Cleveland.*[9]

Pope was encouraging, in his way, to Mrs Allen and, when writing in May 1740, looked forward to the completion of the gardens so that attention could be given to "Mrs Allen's Grotto and Cascade" and he wrote again in August that year to "rejoice extraordinarily that Mrs Allen has begun to imitate the Great Works of Nature, rather than those Bawbles most Ladies affect".[10]

An arch in tufa stone is all that remains of the Grotto

44

Pope spent a good deal of time collecting specimens, and building his grotto at Twickenham. Many of his letters to Allen between 1739 and 1743 contained requests for more stone from the Combe Down quarries to which Allen readily responded, and there are similar letters to William Borlase. In return he sent the Allens pineapples and guinea fowl. Although encouraging to Mrs Allen, it is unclear just how much he was able or allowed to help her. In August 1741, he wrote:

I am as desirous you should see my finish'd Works, as you that I should see yours. To mine you have contributed much, to yours I can contribute little.[11]

He was still working on his grotto in 1743 when he wrote to Allen:

I hope whenever Mrs Allen begins her works of that sort [a grotto], *they will be sooner brought to perfection, and I will attend them as diligently as my own.*[12]

It is not known exactly when the structure, now known as Pope's Grotto, was built and it is not shown on Thorp and Overton's Survey of c.1758. Although only an arch remains, constructed of a strange stone of sponge-like appearance, at one time it was roofed and the 1828 plan shows a rectangular form. The diary entry of a pupil at Bishop Baines' Seminary in 1836 reads:

The roof and sides of this sweet retreat presented to the eye such a dazzling assemblage of shells, fossils, minerals etc. as perfectly astonished us . . . The floor was almost as beautiful as the roof, being composed of a curious kind of stone perforated and inlaid with pine-cones, fragments of bone etc., arranged in tasteful forms and the whole place exhibiting such a profusion of ornament and such a combination of taste and skill as I had never before witnessed.[13]

As we have seen from the brief explanation of the geology of the park, there was a great deal of water associated with the site, emerging as springs at various points. There were probably a number of these channels following the fall of the land down to the fishponds and many visitors mention the waterfalls. Samuel Richardson, the 1748 editor of Defoe's *Tour through the whole Island of Great Britain*, includes them:

Below the House, the gardens were laid out on two terraces and two slopes; but all these are adorned with vases, ornaments and other Stonework; and the affluence of water is so great that it is received in three places; and after many agreeable little falls, at the head of one is a statue of Moses, down to his knees, in an attitude expressive of the admiration he must have shown after striking the rock and seeing the water gush out of it.[14]

The statue of Moses is thought by most writers to have been erected in 1741 and Alexander Pope is said to have made an inscription on its base. The statue continued to excite many of Prior Park's visitors, and the scene conjured up by Richardson is much more in line with Pope's feeling for the Augustan spirit of the age. In particular, as Peter Martin says, this scene of spring, falls and rustic stonework seems to be derived from Pope's commitment in gardening to the classical *locus amoenus*. Many of the classical poets wrote of this classic image of a rocky cave, and the connotations that this would have had for the literati of the day were significant. Undoubtedly, water – in its various forms – was the element in garden design most talked of and written about at the time. An 1839 lithograph of the statue of Moses, although said to be in the garden at Widcombe Manor House, shows water gushing from the rock, down to a pool of water below, and exactly fits Richardson's description of the grounds. Six years later in 1754, Dr Richard Pococke, in his *Travels through England*, writes of a statue of Moses sited above a cascade.[15]

The Lithograph of the Moses statue above a cascade and pool, by Moseley in 1839

These water effects would have pleased Pope and reminded him of the Venus' Vale at Rousham. This, then, would seem to be the scene at the site of the grotto which Mrs Allen planned and executed – with the ideas of her husband's friend. It also marks the grave of Allen's Great Dane puppy, a present from Pope in 1739. A stone slab in the floor beneath the archway has inscribed on it the epitaph:

> *Weep not,*
> *Tread lightly my grave,*
> *Call me pet.*

Pope was also interested in growing rather exotic plants, and there is reference in the letters to a greenhouse being constructed; pineapples were successfully cultivated with the help of John Serle from Twickenham and Lord Burlington's gardener, Henry Scot, an expert on growing this fruit. The earliest record of the pineapple coming into cultivation in this country was around 1720. Sir Matthew Decker and his gardener, Henry Telende, were the first successful producers, and James Brydges – later to become Duke of Chandos – at his second estate at Shaw Hall, Berkshire, grew and sold pineapples at half a guinea each in the 1730s. Pope, as horticulturalist, was interested in the art of growing pineapples, and John Serle was duly growing them at Twickenham. Henry Scot was commended by Pope to Allen as having "a design which I think a very good one, to make Pineapples cheaper in a year or two".[16] Quite where the greenhouses were sited is difficult to say, although they were probably close to the house. It seems that Ralph Allen had expressed some apprehension as to the effects of smoke near the mansion. The greenhouses needed to be heated and Pope wrote to reassure Allen that "there need be no fires all the day, and the quantity [of smoke] . . . so small, that it evaporates within a few yards".[17] It may have been near the Gardener's House or near where the farm buildings were later built. Allen also grew oranges of various types and lemons at Prior Park. If Henry Scot visited Prior Park, as is implied by Pope in his letters, then as Burlington's gardener he would have brought his good experience to Prior Park and its gardens. No doubt he had worked under the direction of William Kent during the 1730s at Chiswick, and would probably have passed on some of the principles of a Kent garden to Dodsley.

From what is known of Pope's interest and attitudes to landscape design, it seems reasonable to surmise that the area of wood on the western side of the lawn was the place that took most of Pope's attention. Thorp's 1742 map shows a rather stylised presentation, but this was a time of rapid change in the Prior Park estate, probably a response to the many influences that were raining down on Allen and his garden staff. There is no doubt of Pope's feeling for water. Kent's Venus' Vale at Rousham and Sherborne had impressed on him what was possible, and the cascade from the statue of Moses higher up the slope was just the start. In the 1740s, the carriage road in front of the mansion did not exist and the cascade could have tumbled down to a serpentine lake in the glade of the wood. At the eastern end of the serpentine was a false bridge, a stone arched structure which allowed the pool of water to pass underneath, and looked from a distance like a small bridge with the hint of a lake or stream issuing beyond.

A photograph taken in 1946 of the Sham Bridge, backed by mature trees

Pococke, writing after a visit in October 1754, sums up the idyllic scene:

> *On the 15th, I saw Mr Allen's gardens, which are laid out in wilderness, with a piece of water in the middle, from which there is a descent, on each side of which are beautiful meadows arising up the hill; on one side is a new Gothick building, higher up a statue of Moses with his hand striking the rock, and below it a beautiful cascade falls down about twenty feet, a little higher is a building of the Cold Bath. The centre of the gardens commands a fine view of Bath.*[18]

Pope's association with Kent and knowledge of his work at Rousham at this time, would have helped him in the design for this area, although equally, as Peter Martin suggests, this part of the garden is probably that closest to his fundamental 'poetic' approach, based as it is on antiquity and allusion. In this area were all the elements revered by the golden age. The garden at Sherborne (Lord Digby's estate) was also an influence; the Prior Park Sham Bridge is said to resemble the rustic bridge at Sherborne. William Kent, who altered Rousham during 1738–39, had used the serpentine line to give canals and lakes a 'natural shape'. In Walpole's words "the gentle stream was taught to serpentine seemingly at its pleasure".[19]

Pope only managed to visit the Allens at Prior Park 6 times although all but the first of his visits were usually of three or four months' duration. He and Ralph Allen corresponded regularly in between, but only 7 years elapsed from his first visit to his last. He died in 1744, but in that short time had seen this corner of the park successfully executed to the Augustan rule of taste and, even by the time of his death, the landscape design was sufficiently mature to enable a visitor to Prior Park to write in 1746:

> *The natural beauties of wood, water and prospect, hill and dale, wilderness and cultivation, make it one of the most delightful spots I ever saw, without adding anything from art. The elegance and judgement with which art has been employed, and the affectation of false grandeur carefully avoided, make one wonder how it could be so busy there without spoiling anything received from nature.*[20]

1. *Correspondence*; op.cit., vol. 4, p. 206.
2. *Correspondence*; op.cit., vol. 4, p. 239.
3. Martin; op.cit., p. 217.
4. Jones, Richard; *A Life* (MS in Bath Reference Library).
5. *Correspondence*; op.cit., vol. 4, p. 452.
6. Peach, R.E.M.; *Life and Times of Ralph Allen*, p. 114 (D. Nutt, London, 1895).
7. Jones, Barbara; *Follies and Grottoes*, p. 34 (London, 1953).
8. Jones, Barbara; op.cit., p. 35.
9. Quoted in Grigson, Geoffrey; *Before the Romantics – An Anthology of the Enlightenment*, p. 183 (Salamander Press, Edinburgh, 1984).
10. *Correspondence*; op.cit., vol. 4, p. 254.
11. *Correspondence*; op.cit., vol. 4, p. 360.
12. *Correspondence*; op.cit., vol. 4, p. 443.
13. Quoted in Duke, Katy; *The Garden Buildings of Prior Park* (unpublished thesis, B. Arch., University of Bath, 1982).
14. Defoe; op.cit.
15. Pocock, Dr. Richard; *The Travels through England*, 1754, p. 153 (Camden Society, 1889).
16. *Correspondence*; op.cit., vol. 4, p. 360.
17. *Correspondence*; op.cit., vol. 4, p. 429.
18. Pococke; op. cit., p. 153.
19. Quoted in Hunt and Willis; op.cit., p. 314.
20. Letter from Charles Yorke to Rev. William Warburton, 30th September 1746, published in *Letters of a Late Eminent Prelate to One of His Friends* (London, 1793).

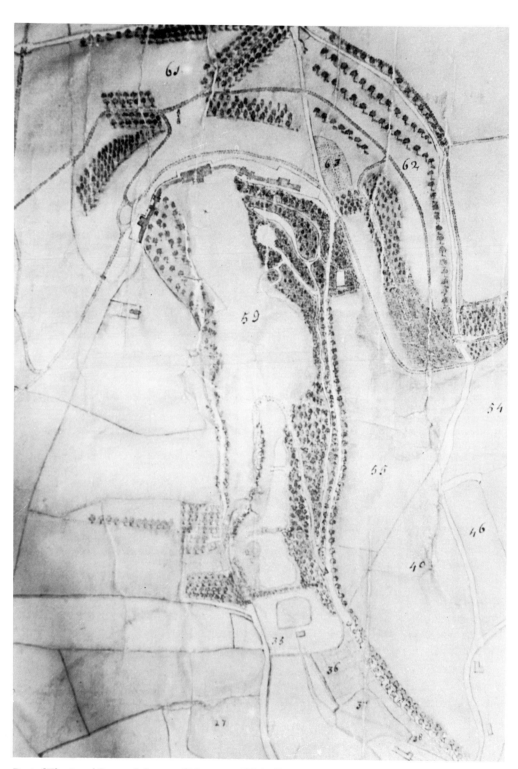

Part of Thorp and Overton's Survey of Manors, c. 1758-63

6 – Surveying and Making Plans

 Once the Allens were settled in their new home, they kept more or less open house to visitors of ability and distinction, and Prior Park became known as a place where interest in the arts flourished, at a time when Bath itself was still attracting the moneyed aristocracy, intent on having an exciting, but not especially cultural, time. Among Allen's guests were Henry Fielding, who lived at Twerton for a while when writing *Tom Jones*, and his sister, Sarah, also a novelist. Samuel Richardson and the painters, Gainsborough and Hoare, were also frequent visitors, as were David Garrick and James Quin. Fielding had a great deal of admiration for Allen and modelled his character of Squire Allworthy on him and the Allworthy estate on Prior Park. The novel contains a description of the estate which is very close to the scene at Prior Park. Fielding also refers to Prior Park itself as a place where

nature appears in her richest attire, and art dressed with the modest simplicity attends her benignant mistress. Here nature indeed pours forth the choicest treasure which she hath lavished on this world.[1]

Samuel Richardson in *The History of Sir Charles Grandison* also used Prior Park and includes a description closely according with the estate.

A great many other visitors were drawn to the estate. The Park was opened to the public on Thursday afternoons in an effort to control the sightseers and, as Boyce says, protect Allen himself from untoward invasion, and must have attracted tourists from the daily round at the Assembly Rooms. Prior Park must have fast become a landmark in Bath, a place to visit, a place worthy of note in many a diarist's hand. Anthony Walker made an engraving showing a perspective of Prior Park which was first published in 1750 and re-printed a number of times. It shows a central dammed pond or basin very much in the position one might imagine to correspond with the "bason" of Wood's design, and with the pond as shown on the 1742 map by Thorp. John Wood had left Allen's employ in 1748, and clerk of works Richard Jones had taken on many of the responsibilities for the mansion which Wood might otherwise have had. The Walker engraving shows a mansion with freestanding wings

51

and pavilions in perfect symmetry, very much in accord with Wood's design. However, there were in fact many departures from the original drawings as the mansion was built. Work had begun in 1735 on the west wing, and the west porte-cochère pavilion and the mansion house were mostly complete by 1748. But Richard Jones altered the east wing during the building stage and so destroyed the balance of Wood's design. So here is the first dilemma: why does Walker show, in 1750, a symmetrical façade resembling Wood's design?

The western woodland is shown by Walker with paths winding through it and a natural irregular edge onto the lawn although this seems to be separated at the northern end, near the "bason", by a fence or wall. The lawn narrows considerably from being the width of the mansion plus the colonnades, to the same width as the "bason", which is presumably fed by unseen streams and rivulets. (Pope observed on perspective: "you may distance things by . . . narrowing the plantation more and more toward the end, in the same manner as they do in painting".[2]) To the east of the lawn there is what appears to be a kitchen garden with paths and neat rows of plants between, screened from the lawn by a hedge punctuated with stone urns on pedestals. This area bears

A watercolour sketch of the central lawn and possible cascade by Thomas Robins, c. 1758

only tenuous resemblance to Thorp's depiction of this side of the lawn in 1742. It could have been that the layout was not settled when Thorp was preparing his plan or that Allen's plans changed in the intervening years. It is unlikely that a plantation would have been felled and cleared in the time. Significantly, the 1750 garden as depicted by Walker, was not unlike the descriptions written of Pope's garden at Twickenham. It is possible that Walker was sketching ideas for Pope for the redesigning of the garden.

A later print by Thomas Robins, drawn in 1758, shows in a view from the fishponds, a central cascade bordered on each side by shrubs or young trees. Allen was then busy with new projects for the landscaping. A letter of 1755 from Rev. William Warburton to Rev. Richard Hurd mentions that he (Allen) had "turned a rich fruit grove into a fine flowery lawn" and hints of his own (Warburton's) distrust in "the caprice of taste or fashion" that caused these changes.[3]

There is no doubt that some fashions of the time were certainly shortlived, and there is known to be stone culverting below the central part of the lawn. Whether this was the full-blown cascade that Robins depicts, or whether Robins had drawn up an idea of what a proposed cascade might look like, is another of the imponderables that this fascinating landscape still contains.

In 1755, Allen was to commission the feature by which Prior Park is most often remembered, the Palladian Bridge. As Boyce says "lighter and more exquisite in design than the great mansion presiding over the scene . . . mysteriously satisfying in its proportions, the bridge was the jewel of Allen's estate".[4]

Plan and elevation of the Palladian Bridge, shown in the margin of Survey of Manours

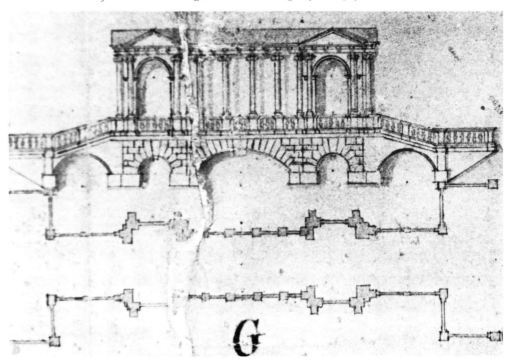

Its direct model was a similar bridge at Wilton House, built by the ninth Earl of Pembroke around 1735–37, the only difference being the slightly wider spacing between the centre columns. At the same time as this bridge was planned, the fishponds were enlarged to roughly the size we find them today and I suspect that the Palladian bridge and associated works may have been part of the "caprice of fashion" that Warburton wrote of so disparagingly. The architect for the bridge is unknown; some historians suggest it to be the design of John Wood the Elder, but he had died in 1754, or it could simply have been a straightforward copy of the bridge at Wilton. The working drawings are claimed to have been drawn up by Richard Jones. Others suggest Lancelot 'Capability' Brown. This is based on a reference in Humphrey Repton's *Landscape Gardening*, that in 1765 Brown designed an additional feature for Allen. Brown was not known to have been working anywhere in the vicinity of Bath until he was at Bowood in 1757, and it is most likely to have been an inspired copy by Richard Jones.

The bridge first appears in the Robins drawing of 1758 and again on Thorp and Overton's map of c.1758, and visitors begin to make mention of the bridge in correspondence about the same time. Thomas Potter, a frequent visitor to Prior Park in the mid-1750s and by then Joint Vice-Treasurer for Ireland, was probably introduced to the Allens by William Pitt. In May 1755, he wrote to Pitt:

> *the scenes at Prior Park change every hour . . . The present joy at the birth of an heir* [Gertrude Warburton, Allen's niece, gave birth to a son, Ralph, on 1st May], *does not respite the labours of the gardener. Half the summer will show the bridge, the dairy opens to the lake; vast woods have taken possession of the naked hills; and the lawns slope uninterrupted to the valleys.*[5]

This letter confirms the activity in the landscape around this time and could also be taken as indicating a change in the appearance of the central lawn. In a sense, the Palladian bridge brings together the influence of the two most important men (in terms of taste) at Prior Park. Here we have the bridge derived from Palladio no less, John Wood's theoretical mentor and guide, used, as Pope would have wanted, as a landscape feature to be appreciated from a distance. A river or piece of water, so necessary to the landscape would also require a bridge but, in order to 'read' pictorially, the ideal bridge needed height as well as span, and a superstructure of some kind. Palladio illustrates two bridges of this sort in his *Third Book of Architecture* of 1570 and points to the Pons Aelius in ancient Rome, the approach to Hadrian's Mausoleum, as the forerunner, but there were also the medieval bridges with gatehouses, and later houses perched along the road as on the Ponte Vecchio in Florence. Palladio produced a design for the Rialto Bridge in Venice with these characteristics although on a much larger scale than the English derivative. It was probably Lord Pembroke who was responsible for anglicising this idea and

The Lodge built by Ralph Allen in a Gothic style, on the fields to the east of the mansion

using it to such good fortune within the English Landscape Garden. Pope, too, would have liked this pedigree for an architectural feature of this nature.

The first plan that shows the Palladian Bridge is the *Survey of the Manours of Ralph Allen* carried out by Thorp and Overton probably around 1758, although the exact date has not been determined.[6] This is an important reference work, showing not only the whole of Allen's land holdings, but also the Prior Park estate in detail. The most startling difference to the previous drawings and maps is the 'natural' style of the park that the landscape has assumed. Gone are the straight lines of Walker, gone too is the kitchen garden and, instead, trees are shown scattered along the eastern side the lawn. There is no hint of a central cascade, and although the western grove of trees still has its twisting paths, there is now also a serpentine lake, and a clearing in the trees. On the south side of the mansion, the avenues of trees are clearly maturing and, from the road junction where the Upper Lodge now stands, a drive leads through trees to the eastern wing where the offices were situated. There are also drives leading on to the adjoining Lodge Field (now known as Monument Field), where the Allens erected a lodge in the Gothic style.

The survey of Thorp and Overton is accompanied by plans and sketches of the main garden buildings, which must have existed at the time. The lodge is illustrated along with the other named buildings already discussed: the Palladian Bridge, the Gardener's House, the Sham Bridge, and also some others – a Castle on the Warren (Sham Castle), the Dairy House, the Thatch'd House, the Cold Bath and the Gothic Temple in the Woods.

The Cold Bath could be the building shown on the earlier Walker engraving situated closer to the house surrounded by trees on the eastern side. There is, however, always the possibility that this building was the greenhouse for the pineapples, over which Pope took so much trouble. A plan prepared much later in 1856, names this building, however, as a 'Bath House'. The Thatch'd House is another unknown. No location is pinpointed on any map of the period or later and it does not seem to be mentioned by any visitors. Peter Martin speculates on the possibility that this little structure with its stone walls and thatched roof may have been Mrs Allen's grotto, even though it was clearly identified in her lifetime as the Thatch'd House. The wood-engraving of 1800 of the Gothic Temple in the Woods is also confusingly entitled the Grotto.

Near the fishponds, close to the western boundary, an indistinct circular shape is indicated on the Thorp and Overton survey. It is possible that this, too, could have been the location of the Thatch'd House, although on the 1856 plan it is clearly marked as an 'Ice House'.

We have already discovered that there were a number of Gothic-styled buildings on the Prior Park estate. The Gardener's House, in its safe and solid style, owing much to the Gothic style of Wren, was to lead to something much more delicate. William Kent was to be the landscape architect who epitomised and developed the flimsy, decorative characteristics of the Gothic style to something unmistakably Georgian – as Summerson suggests, it was a matter "of selecting Gothic features which appealed to him [Kent] as characteristic and decorative and then arranging them conformably to his classically trained taste".[7] The Gothic Temple – built by Richard Jones in 1745 – is characterised by similar pretty and delicate features, but although Kent's style was popular and widely known, it is unlikely that his designs were adopted for this building.

The Gothic Temple, dscribed as a Chapel on this postcard of the early 1900s. The tiled, pitched roof was an alteration to the original design.

56

More probably, one of the many architectural pattern books of the time, like the one published by Batty Langley in 1742, would have been used. There were numerous pattern books of the mid 18th century; Campbell and Leoni had started something with their works on architecture, and there were several other works on the design of buildings, and gardens. Between 1725 and 1760 there was at least one such treatise published per year, many aimed at the country gentleman and his builder.

Besides the fashion for Gothic, there was also a taste for the Chinese and several books of Chinese design were published, the first of which, *New Designs for Chinese Temples*, appeared in 1750. Walpole mentions some buildings at Wroxton in 1753 as being the first of their kind. The Chinese Gate, or Rock Gate, along the western boundary of the estate links with the heavily retained track which leads from high above the fishponds to the opposite side of the combe. The location is shown clearly on the Thorp and Overton survey of c.1758, but it is not until 1913 that it is actually given the name Rock Gate. From its design, however, it could have been made about the time when foreign influences periodically drifted across Palladian England.

The fashion for Gothic continued to develop quite strongly in England but at the same time the thinking on perception of beauty was developing, no less in landscape design, as in other areas of art. William Hogarth set out to analyse beauty and list its qualities, and the influence of the painters like Claude, Poussin and Salvator Rosa began to be widely known, with landowners striving to achieve the same effects. The romantic ruin was an incident of such scenes, and writers on this 'Picturesque' landscape, such as William Gilpin, frequently refer to these artificial ruins that had become popular features in the landscape.

The Chinese gate near the Middle Lodge on Ralph Allen Drive

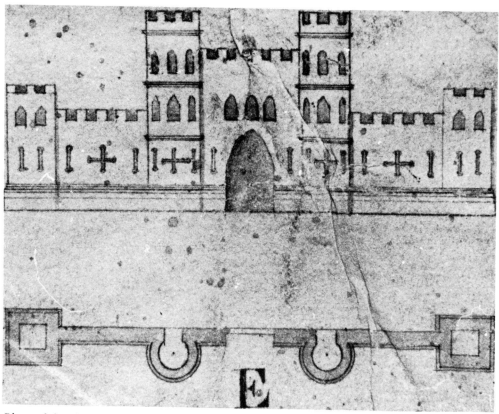

Plan and elevation of the Sham Castle, as shown on the Thorp and Overton Survey, c. 1758

Allen's friend, William Pitt, M.P. for Bath, was instrumental in arranging for Sanderson Miller, the amateur architect, to design a "very considerable Gothic Object which is to stand in a very fine situation on the Hills near Bath".[8] Allen must have known of the Gothic ruin at Stowe, and of the Sham Castle built by Miller for Lord Lyttleton at Hagley. Richard Jones records that in 1762, Allen began the Castle on the Warren, where previously fir trees had been planted, and it now stands, not, interestingly, as an ornament for the inhabitants of the Prior Park mansion, but visible from Allen's town house and a sight for the Bath visitors. Barbara Jones refers to it as "utterly unreal, a cardboard fort in a toyshop".[9] Both William Pitt and Sanderson Miller were familiar with Henry Fielding's allusion to Allen in *Tom Jones* and the descriptions of Squire Allworthy's estate as having a view "on the right . . . of one of the towers of an old ruined abbey, grown over with ivy and part of the front which remained still entire".[10] As Boyce suggests, they would probably have enjoyed the idea of helping Allen to look more like his written portrait.

To return to the question of 'Capability' Brown, and the possibilities of his visiting Prior Park, after Allen's death in 1764, a bill from Brown is recorded in the estate's accounts for £60.0.0d. for surveying and making plans. There are no surviving survey plans of this date nor any further information which can help with this problem. However, there are a number of connections of the estate with Brown. William Pitt and Brown had met at Stowe and were on friendly terms for over 40 years. Pitt had been a frequent visitor to Stowe during the 1740s when Brown was employed by Lord Cobham. When Pitt inherited a mansion in Somerset at Burton Pynsent in the 1770s, it was to Brown that he turned to ask for a design of a commemorative column in the park. Pitt was, of course, also a good friend of Ralph Allen and it would not be surprising if the recommendation of Brown had passed between them. Many authorities consider the landscape at Prior Park to have been the work of Brown from its character. I would suggest, however, that the lawn, woodland and the Palladian Bridge had been of that character for some time by the 1760s and that, if Brown had worked for Ralph Allen earlier, there would be more records or letters available. A survey costing £60.0.0d., even in the 1760s, would not have extended very far. Some suggest that he may have surveyed a particular aspect, for example, the watercourses, but we must remember that Allen's property spread over hundreds of acres, and the survey may have been of an area which did not form part of the Prior Park estate immediate to the mansion. For the time being, at least, the object of the £60.0.0d. bill will remain an enigma.

Ralph Allen died in June 1764 and was buried in Claverton churchyard. Elizabeth Allen died two years later and Prior Park became the property of Gertrude Warburton (Allen's niece) who had married the future Bishop in 1745.

1. Fielding, Henry; *Tom Jones*, p. 545 (Penguin Books, Harmondsworth, 1966).
2. Spence; op.cit., p. 610.
3. Letter from Rev. William Warburton to Rev. Richard Hurd, March 1755, published in *Letters of a Late Eminent Prelate to One of His Friends* (London, 1793).
4. Boyce; op.cit., p. 189.
5. Quoted by Boyce; op.cit., p. 232.
6. The exact dates of the survey and plans of Thomas Thorp and John Overton are uncertain. The plan is thought to have been made between 1758 and 1763.
7. Summerson; op.cit., pp. 398-9.
8. Quoted by Boyce; op.cit., p. 226, from a correspondence of William Pitt to Sanderson Miller in October 1755.
9. Jones, Barbara; op.cit., p. 75.
10. Fielding; op.cit., pp. 58-9.

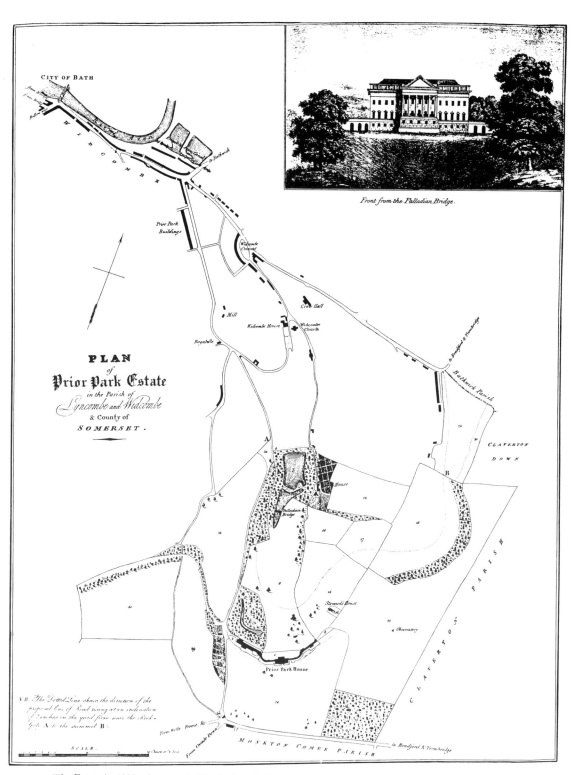

Front from the Palladian Bridge.

CITY OF BATH

W I D C O M B E

Prior Park
Buildings

Widcombe
Crescent

Mill

Widcombe House

Widcombe
Church

Crew Hall

Bagatelle

Bathwick Parish

PLAN
of
Prior Park Estate
in the Parish of
Lyncombe and Widcombe
& County of
SOMERSET.

CLAVERTON
DOWN

House

Palladian
Bridge

CLAVERTON PARISH

Stewards House

Observatory

Prior Park House

N.B. The Dotted Line shews the direction of the
proposed line of Road rising at an inclination
of 2 inches in the yard from near the Road
Gate A to the summit B.

SCALE.

MONKTON COMBE PARISH

The Estate in 1828 when acquired by Bishop Baines

7 – Perhaps the Finest View in the Kingdom

 The Warburtons stayed only a short while. William Warburton was ambitious to be granted a bishopric and he was soon to be given the See at Gloucester. After Allen's death, Gertrude had demolished the Gothic lodge above Rainbow Wood, much to the distress of Mrs Allen (who seems to have liked the building) and to the annoyance of Richard Jones;

> *She* [Gertrude] *caused to be pulled down one of the neatest gothic piles of buildings which stood in the Lodge field which Mr Allen took a great deal of notice of to all gentlemen that came, – to show it, from it was an exceedingly fine prospect into Wales and Wiltshire and Somersetshire.*[1]

Later, the Warburtons put up in its place a monument to the memory of Ralph Allen, a curious building with a circular turret on a Gothic-style triangular base. However, there were problems with the estate. Allen had made a number of bequests which had to be paid. On his death, the postal business was taken over by the Postmaster General and, although Philip Allen, Ralph's nephew, was retained as a Comptroller of the Cross-Road and Bye Posts Office, his salary and that of other staff was greatly reduced. The effect of this loss of revenue was not anticipated by the Warburtons; moreover, they had increasing commitments in Gloucester. In 1769, Gertrude therefore decided to leave the estate, to sell off the contents and lease the mansion. (There were legal restraints which prevented an outright sale.) Richard Jones was even more dismayed.

The former glories of Prior Park as a place of meeting for literary men was, in 1769, suddenly at an end. For the next 60 years the estate had a variety of tenants and owners living there, some of whom, but not all, cared for the landscape. At the auction most of the domestic contents were sold – furniture, china and porcelain, linen, kitchen equipment. So too were 240 sheep, 80 lambs and 4 rams, 8 horses, 10 cows and the harnesses and paraphernalia from the coach houses, large numbers of garden chairs, a pile of fir faggots

The engraving of Prior Park by Thomas Hearne

(in the Park) and a parcel of oak timber (at Combe Down). Some of the quarrying equipment – a stone carriage, 2 broad-wheeled carts and 2 narrow-wheeled waggons and the cranes from the docks at Dolemead – were also sold.

After the sale, the mansion was leased to Francis Fitzmaurice, third Earl of Kerry, but not for long. In 1779, Bishop Warburton died and Gertrude married his chaplain, the Rev. Stafford Smith. By 1785 she had returned to live at Prior Park, now as Mrs Smith. A fine engraving by Thomas Hearne commemorates her occupancy and shows the mansion looking probably at its best. Fifty years on from the first plantings, the landscape was maturing, and the avenue of trees on the south side framed the building. The Park continued to be a draw for visitors and Collinson comments favourably on it in 1791, referring to it as "stately" . . . and "magnificent".[2] He goes on:

> *This house is acknowledged to command perhaps the finest view in the kingdom; and from its lofty situation, the magnificence of its portico, and its general appearance, affords a splendid object to the city of Bath and its environs.*

He also writes of Combe Down and describes the quarry workers' cottages which by then were let to invalids from Bath,

who retire for the sake of the very fine air (probably rendered more salubrious by the plantation of firs) . . . The surrounding beautiful and extensive prospects; the wild but pleasing irregularities of the surface and scenery, diversified with immense quarries, fine open cultivated fields and extensive plantations of firs [those planted by Allen] which throw a solemn gloominess of shade impervious to the sun and winds, over a fine soft turf free from underwood; all serve to render this a delightful summer retreat.[3]

On Gertrude Smith's death in 1796 the property passed to Cornwallis Maude, widower of another of Ralph Allen's nieces, Mary (Ralph's brother Philip's only daughter). Maude was created Baron de Montalt in 1785 (of de Montalt paper mills in Combe Down) and had become in 1793, Viscount Hawarden. His son inherited in 1803 but he died soon after, in 1807, without an heir. The connection with Ralph Allen was finally severed.

After a few years, the estate was occupied by John Thomas, a Quaker from Bristol who seems to invite variable criticism of the care he took in the maintenance of the landscape. Pierce Egan, in his *Walks through Bath* of 1819, says

. . . on the left side of the road, the pleasure-grounds beneath, belonging to Prior-House, appear in fine cultivation; and the water, and the foliage of the chesnut [sic], fir and elm trees increase the effect.[4]

On the other hand, Monsignor James Shepherd, writing in 1894 mainly about Prior Park College, casts doubt on the family's management of the estate.

From the year 1817, the domain and Mansion, during the occupancy of a Mr. Thomas, suffered much from parsimonious neglect; and a fine avenue of valuable trees in the present playground was cut down with the object of turning the timber into money.[5]

On the death of John Thomas, the leasehold of the estate was again up for sale. These sale particulars of 1828 make a very useful checklist and timely description, indicating how well in fact the features of the estate had survived.[6] The park-like grounds were "ornamented with an obelisk", probably that of Marshal Wade. The grounds seem to have been in good condition, "richly adorned with thriving timber and evergreens, extensive walks and rides", with the main lawn framing the view to the north, "a very beautiful Dell, skirted each side with trees of great variety, size and beauty". The grotto, an "alcove" and "several cascades" are listed; so too is the Palladian bridge. The lawn is fenced off from the house and used for pasture; the Priory Cottage (described as a *cottage orné*) is also surrounded by pasture land. The Farm House, with gardens of about an acre, is near the fishponds, and the kitchen gardens were to the west of the carriage drive, "fully stocked, cropped and planted, walled

Thomas Robins' drawing of the Monument erected by Bishop Warburton, in memory of Ralph Allen. It was demolished in 1953.

and cross-walled, clothed with numerous choice fruit trees, springs of fine clear water, and ponds, dry gravelled walks, alcove etc.". The farmyard was next to the stable wing and the land to the south of the mansion, described as the "park", was also out to pasture. The estate in all comprised around 198 acres.

Dr. Peter Augustine Baines first came to Bath in 1817 to run the Benedictine mission. During his stay he visited Prior Park and must have noted its potential. In 1823 he was appointed as the Assistant Bishop for the Western District of the Catholic Church, but became ill. It was while he was convalescing in Rome that he gained experience of the architecture of antiquity (he was already a classical scholar) and was able to see at first hand some of the grandiose schemes in Italy. These ideas were surely in his mind when he later returned to England in 1829 to take up promotion as Bishop for the District. The Roman Catholic church was organised into 4 districts in England and Wales at that time. The Western District covered Wales as well as the west and south-west of England, but had only a small catholic population. Baines was an able, cultured and ambitious man. He was as anxious as any that the Western District should have a seminary for training priests, and he saw Prior Park as a very suitable place for it, where all Bath could witness the growth in importance of the Catholic community. Late in the same year Baines completed the purchase of Prior Park at a price of £22,000.

His ideas for the seminary, and for a college for the general education of catholic boys, involved considerable additions to the existing buildings on site. Baines brought in the local architect, H. E. Goodridge, to help. Work started on the eastern wing, named St. Peter's, which was to be the seminary. To the central block of this wing an extra storey was added and the *porte-cochère* was converted to Baines' private oratory. In the base of this pavilion was a lecture theatre. Additions were built along both sides of the wing altering the elevations that had been designed by Jones. The western wing saw even more changes. There was a narrow addition to the north elevation and all the stables and coach houses were altered. Shepherd comments:

> *the classrooms at St. Paul's* [the western wing] *are only a modification of the stables and cow-houses, but so admirably adapted, and so handsome in their proportions, that it is impossible to trace in them the humble purposes to which they were formerly put.*[7]

An extra floor was also added to this wing. These alterations were completed around 1831, although Baines is said to have disliked the smooth stone finish on the western wing. He therefore had the masons chisel the stone into apparent blocks, giving the St. Paul's wing the appearance of being constructed of huge blocks of stone in a rusticated manner. The coach-house, between the stables and Wood's original *porte-cochère*, was converted into a billiards room.

Baines then had the inspiration of adding a magnificent flight of steps to the north elevation of the mansion. Baines had an eye for ceremony and spectacle, and is said to have wanted to publicise the grandeur of open air processions, for example on Palm Sunday or Corpus Christi. Goodridge designed the steps in 1834. Not all members of the seminary seemed to be quite so enthusiastic as Baines. Shepherd again:

> *let us not imagine that these magnificent flights of steps started into existence without much labour and expense. It would be difficult to estimate the cost of them; but some idea may be gained by considering the large area over which they stretch.*[8]

Shepherd goes on to explain the considerable earth-moving operation that was necessary. The terracing had to be extended to accommodate the double flight, and a grand sweep had to be made to correspond to the lower flight. Excavations were taking place on the southern front to the buildings so, for-

*A print of 1830 showing the North Front before
alterations by Bishop Baines*

tunately, plenty of earth was available. In order to make room for the additions
to the wings, a considerable volume of earth had to be dug out. Previously
the land behind the colonnades came sloping down to within 4 feet of the
buildings, terminated by a low wall about three feet high. Shepherd also
mentions 4 urns which decorate the steps. [9] One of the students of the college,
Luke Metcalfe, on hearing the masons grumbling one day, took up the chisel
and carved "a very respectable foliated vase" to show what could be done. He
evidently proceeded to finish all four, to the masons' chagrin.

It was probably at this time that the carriage driveway on the north side of
the mansion was constructed. The steps would logically have swept down to
the driveway, providing a grand ceremonial entrance to the mansion. It is
shown on engravings from about 1836.

Goodridge and Baines between them had plans for a magnificent church
with a high dome sited to the south of the mansion on what is now the playing
fields. This would have had enormous consequences for the view of Prior
Park from the city and one cannot help but speculate on what the city fathers,
as well as the Bath population, would have made of it. There must have been
plenty of other proposals. An image, published in 1840, shows even more
substantial buildings, with extra floors added to the wings and to the
colonnades.

66

PRIOR PARK, BATH.

The grand flight of steps and steep embankments, in a print of 1836

The college opened its doors to students in 1830 and the Priory, formerly the Gardener's house, formed the dormitory for the older students, and some of the Professors also had rooms there. When the rooms in St. Paul's were ready, the cottage was let to a succession of tenants, the first of which was the Hon. Miss Crewe, a great benefactress of the college. Later on, G. R. Bryant made some additions to the building "so as to suit the requirements of a large family", with the result that Shepherd is able to describe it as "beautifully decorated and furnished", and "convenient and picturesque".[10] He also comments on the grounds of the Priory. They have "undergone a marvellous change, and the terraces lying one below the other are admirably adapted for outdoor amusements". The 1828 sale particulars' plan shows the Priory surrounded by fields; by 1856, the date of the next sale of Prior Park, the scene has changed to show much more tree planting, enclosing a lawn and at least two "basons" with fountains. The spring which fed these ponds can still be seen today.

Baines also took a great deal of interest in the surroundings and initiated several schemes for tree-planting. He had the aid and advice of an arboriculturalist, a Mr. Knight, who was also a friend. Baines was responsible for the thick band of trees which shelters St. Peter's College from the east winds and for belts of trees around the playing fields. The main species planted were firs, beech and oak.

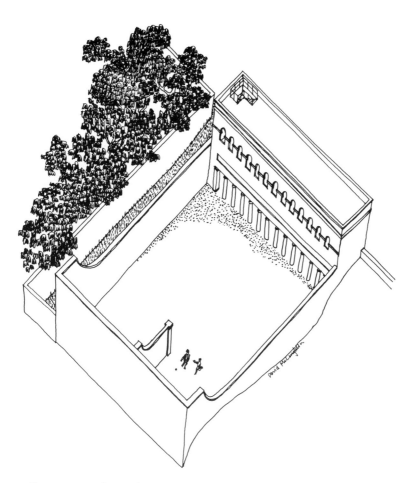

A reconstruction of the Gymnasium

Sport was also a feature of seminary life. Baines had constructed a spacious terrace to the south-east of St. Peter's College, at the end of which is "a very substantial building and ball-place" now know as The Gymnasium. This was erected by Rev. James Baines, nephew to the Bishop. It was probably built around 1840 (the Tithe Map of 1836 omits this building, and James died in 1843, at the tragically early age of 32), and the architect is thought to have been Goodridge again. It was sited in the quarry from which the stones were taken to build it. Shepherd tell us that "the flat-roof was intended originally to serve as a watch tower, from which the Prefect had a commanding view of the 'bounds' and the 'tennis-court' ".[11] The rooms below were intended for "reading rooms in wet weather and for imposition rooms". The ball-place was initially very popular and Brother J. S. Roche, writing the school's history in 1931, says the game of Fives was a popular game in spring and summer.[12]

Cricket was also played, but regarded by some as an "idle pastime". Renewing the wicket, with gravel, was thought a very serious business and every Easter there was this "mighty bother" of renewal. Turf was apparently not considered suitable.

It was always Bishop Baines' idea, too, to build a church for the College and finally a site was chosen – the part of the west wing which had been converted to a billiards room. Unhappily, Baines did not live to see it; he died suddenly in the summer of 1843. He had been the driving force and inspiration for setting the seminary and college successfully in business, and he had overseen some very significant changes to the buildings at Prior Park, and to some extent to the gardens as well. However, his main purpose at Prior Park was education and we are fortunate that this principle was of overriding importance, so that the landscape was allowed to remain largely unchanged. Well-known in the history of Prior Park, the fire of 1836 gutted and badly damaged the mansion and, of Wood's designs, only the chapel remained relatively unscathed. The college was already thought by some to be under-financed. The fire, and the fact that not all the loss was covered by insurance put even greater strain on the finances. However, Baines went ahead with refitting and repairing the damage, and took advantage of the sale of contents of Hunstrete House to restore some of the former glory and add new. With the other extensions, there was little spare money for a church. Nevertheless, bequests from catholic friends were received, enough to start the church if not finish it. Monsignor Thomas Brindle, temporarily in charge of the College after Baines' death, started the building in 1844. He chose Joseph Scoles, who designed a church in the 'Roman' style to suit the rest of the buildings.

In all, some £3,000 came in and "the outside walls reached the requisite elevation". From this time the financial burden on the college and on the Clifton diocese became a threat to the future of Prior Park. Once again in the lifetime of Prior Park, its guardians had underestimated the costs of this large estate. In 1856, the school and seminary closed and the property was auctioned.

1. Jones, Richard; op.cit.
2. Collinson; op.cit., p. 169.
3. Collinson; op.cit., p. 170.
4. Egan, Pierce; *Walks Through Bath*, p. 214 (Mary Meyler and Son, Bath, 1819).
5. Shepherd, Monsignor James; *Reminiscences of Prior Park*, p. 68 (Isaac Pitman and Sons, London, 1894).
6. Sale particulars of 1828 seen at the Clifton Diocesan Archives by kind permission of the Diocesan Archivist.
7. Shepherd; op.cit., p.70.
8. Shepherd; op.cit., p.81.
9. Shepherd; op.cit., p.82.
10. Shepherd; op.cit., p.142.
11. Shepherd; op.cit., p.102.
12. Roche, Rev. Bro. J.S.; *A History of Prior Park College and its Founder Bishop Baines*, p. 285 (Burns, Oates and Washbourne, London, 1931).

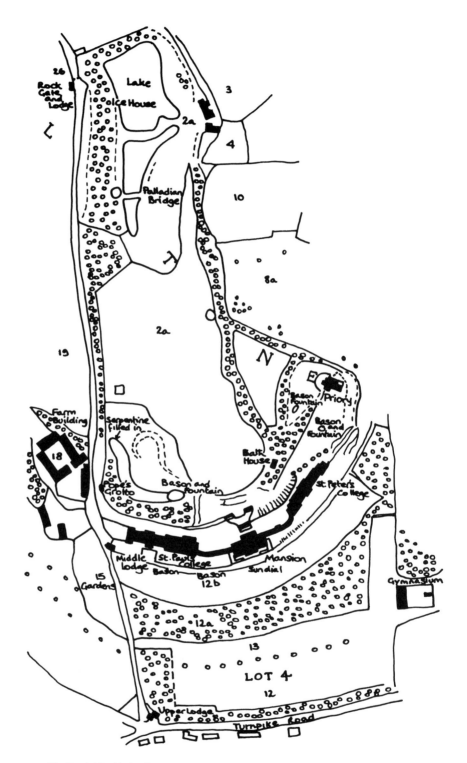

Estate plans prepared by Daniel Smith for the 1856 Auction

8 – For All Bath to See

The Record of Sale of 1856, together with the Plans, provides us with an opportunity to review the state of the buildings of the estate. The Gymnasium is described as containing a covered colonnade, 80ft. by 18ft.; a calefactory; a prefect's room; a reading room; a flagged terrace 80ft. by 18ft.; and a tennis or ball-court 80ft. by 100ft. There was also a gravel terrace, 520ft. by 50ft., and a grass cricket ground of about ten acres. The gravel terrace is something of an enigma – it is believed to have been grassed later and it is likely that its use was in some way linked to that of the Gymnasium. A running or athletics strip has been suggested, as have archery butts or an exercise strip for horses. Various garden artefacts were also sold at the auction, including some statues in Bath stone. Amongst them was a St. Peter sold for £9.9.0; Hercules in repose for £17.6.6; 2 busts of Caesar for £2.0.0; and a draped figure of Flora for £5.0.0. Also listed are columns, a garden seat and a quantity of rustic carved stonework and rock stone. There is no way of knowing for certain whether these statues were from the 18th or 19th century.

There was certainly plenty of statuary in the latter part of the 18th century, and we have already noted that masons were at work in the 19th century embellishing the steps. It is also worth noting that the estate was still very much on the tourist map. The Bath Guide Books mentioned it year in, year out; Dr. James Tunstall, in his *Rambles about Bath*, describes the mansion and grounds (referring to the "well-kept lawns"), and the Gothic monument, which by 1847 was "crumbling through neglect, and promises, for want of slight repairs, to become a ruin".[1] He also mentions that the firs are nearly all gone except inside the park where "they form a delightful walk". The Scots pines were probably planted to shelter the deciduous trees when young. Their disappearance is not too surprising.

At the other end of the estate, the 1856 plan shows a circular ice-house above the fishponds. Nearby, a subterranean passage is indicated. Although it was not unusual to have an ice-house – they had after all been a regular feature of large country house estates since the 17th century, and were very popular by the 19th – the subterranean passage remains an unexplained mystery.

A view of the North front published in 1894

The mansion and estate buildings were empty for a while before Thomas Thompson rented the mansion in 1859. He seems to have been something of a man of benevolent impulses. For the five summers that he lived at Prior Park, he opened the estate in fine weather to school parties, church gatherings and so on, for picnics. Shepherd describes how he enjoyed giving children's treats as often as possible and two or three times a week, parties of children and their parents would come to roam the grounds and play. The whole estate associated with the mansion was opened, tea provided and "in joyous abandonment the children sported on the lawns, whilst their seniors wandered through the shady walks or spacious buildings". [2] The Thompsons seemed to have thoroughly enjoyed themselves and joined in the fun.

During this time, Dr. Clifford was appointed Bishop of Clifton, and the diocesan Grammar School at Clifton Wood in Bristol was expanding. Dr. Edward Williams, the headmaster, and his staff were excited by a proposal to move to Bath, and the Bishop concurred with this idea. He undertook to re-purchase Prior Park and in April 1867, a Roman Catholic Grammar School opened, centred at first on the St. Paul's wing of Prior Park. There is no evidence of great changes to the buildings, as there had been during Bishop Baines' time; the most significant building achievement was the completion of Scoles' church. There is a photograph in Roche's history, of a forlorn looking church interior, open to the sky, with ivy and other vegetation growing at floor level and up the inside walls of the building. Work on the church resumed in 1872 and the architect was the original designer's son, Alexander Joseph Cory Scoles. The interior finishing was again financed by generous benefactions. The church's completion was the final change to Wood's symmetrical design.

It is difficult to detect what attention was given to the maintenance of the grounds. Rev. Francis Kilvert, writing in his diary on 22nd January 1874, evokes a certain air of neglect which does not seem altogether without charm:

> *We went boldly in at the Lodge Gates . . . past the long damp dreary ranges of ugly buildings, half barrack half jail, till we turned the last wing and came round to the garden front and the great portico looking over Bath. The shrubbery . . . overgrown with long neglect. Upon the great stone balustrades of the wide terrace stairs sat four peacocks, one a white bird, a huge white swan lumbered waddling along a grass-grown gravel path on his way down to the lakes in the hollow of the park, and two ecclesiastics in cassocks and birettas tramped up and down the ground terrace-walk smoking, laughing and spitting right and left. Every now and then the strange musical note of a swan sounded like a trumpet from the bushes.*[3]

The 1884 Ordnance Survey shows the Gardener's House transformed to the Priory with a small garden attached

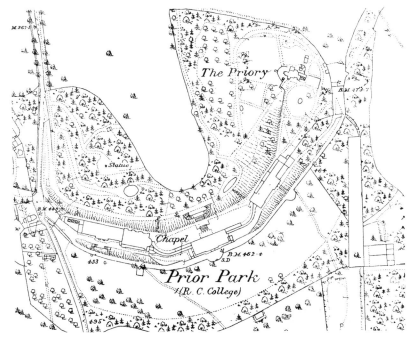

The church, started by Joseph Scoles and completed by his son

The estate had been unattended for at least 11 years and no doubt very little in the way of tree maintenance or replanting had been undertaken. The Surveyors (Cotterell and Spackman) for the Valuation and Sale of 1869 record in the documents the wise observation that much of the timber is "arrived at maturity" and that a "considerable quantity of timber might be advantageously cut without injuring the ornamental character" and that replanting of suitable species should follow.[4] They also comment that the North Lawn was suffering "great injury" due to the shading of the timber, and was therefore of little value. The new school's main concern was education, and keeping the school in business must have taken most of the administrators' energies without the extra concern of the landscape. An entry in Bishop Clifford's diary in 1882 is therefore particularly interesting as it shows the sort of attention that was paid to the estate and farmland

> *Walked over estate at Prior Park with Austin King [the school's solicitor] – to see the clearings made – holes dug for planting 2,000 trees, new fences put up – drinking troughs for cattle, newly arranged so as not to allow sewage to flow into the Ponds – all the drains are being cleaned and mended.[5]*

There was also some tree felling on the estate. Austin King wrote to Bishop Clifford in November 1885, confirming that some trees were to be cut down and that it would take several days.

A belt of planting below the Goodridge steps is shown on the 1884 Ordnance Survey map, but the clearing in the woodland, marked with a statue, the

74

Gothic Temple in the Woods, and the Grotto are still clearly marked. The serpentine lake was reduced to the size of the present pond by 1856. While there was undoubtedly some care and attention given to the landscape at this time, R. E. M. Peach remarked, in the *Life and Times of Ralph Allen*, published in 1895, on the "deterioration in this beautiful estate", apparent especially in the gardens on the north side.[6] They did and still do, however, retain their essentially 18th century structure and form.

Some of the buildings on the estate were not much used, or at least not for their original purpose. We have already read that Ralph Allen's monument was in poor repair. The building known as the Ball-court, now the Gymnasium, was in the 1890s occupied by the "Ground-man" and his wife, who looked after any cases of illness where isolation was advised. Shepherd says that for nearly 40 years – that must be the years of Thompson and of Bishop Clifford's Grammar school – the ball-court remained "alienated from its original purposes" and was at this time used for a poultry yard.[7] The cricket field at last got some attention – the status of the game was gaining. A note in the school magazine in April 1892 records the hard manual work, most of it carried out by the pupils, that had to be undertaken to achieve a cricket pitch of good standard. Previously, presumably, the wicket was of only fair condition, and the outfield was marred by the uneven quarry debris. Bishop Clifford allowed several trees to be cut down, and the writer in the school magazine was hoping that more could be removed so the cricket ground could be of a better size and standard.

The Priory, extended in the late 19th century

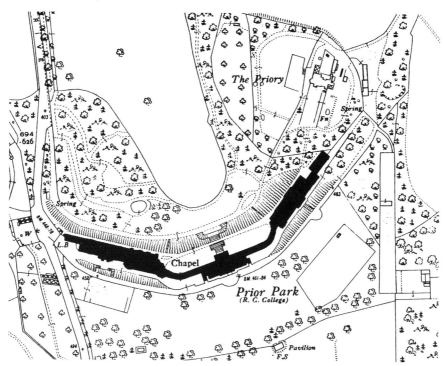

More changes around the Priory shown on the 1936 Ordnance Survey plan

When the headmaster, Monsignor Williams, died in 1891 (followed soon after by Bishop Clifford in 1893) the school yet again ran into financial difficulties. These two men between them had seen the school and its estate revitalised from a wilderness after the Thompson era. Now the school continued until the financial burden became excessive in 1904.

From then until 1921, Prior Park was tenanted by various educational agencies and during the First World War it was occupied by the Army.[8] There were also substantial periods when the premises were empty and inevitably the grounds and buildings suffered from this neglect. A plan was prepared in 1913, probably based on the Ordnance Survey map of 1904, and presumably for one of these many occupiers, by Calvert, Spackman and Son, land agents of Bath.[9] The greatest changes are in the vicinity of the Priory, where the oval lawn and pond of 1884 have been altered to take in a further terrace, producing the attractive lawn with borders that we see today. An orchard is marked on the lower slopes below the Priory although there are no fruit trees remaining now on this particularly wet, steep land. A cottage is shown where the headmaster's house now stands, an enlargement of the shed or outhouse of 1884. The terrace leading to the former Gymnasium is labelled "tennis courts" although it is difficult to arrange modern-sized courts on this land.

After the First World War, Prior Park was controlled by Catholic organisations and housed an industrial school which had moved from Somerset.[10] The Congregation of Irish Christian Brothers took over the property in 1921 and moved the boarders from St. Brendan's College in Bristol. From 1924, a boys' boarding school was established. Many of the buildings were again altered, although they were mainly internal alterations to accommodate the gradual growth of the college. School magazines continue to refer to the tree planting; in 1920, Brother L. Curtin planted a row of Douglas firs by the wall in Ralph Allen Drive, and some poplars were planted opposite Pope's grotto in 1928.

The carriage drive from Widcombe up to the Combe Down quarries was a private gated road, the only access to Prior Park, and had remained so as part of the estate until 1921, when it was acquired by the City Council and renamed Ralph Allen Drive. The 1936 Ordnance Survey map shows few differences from the plan produced in 1913. The statue marked in the clearing within the western plantation no longer appears, nor does the Gothic Temple, noted as the Oratory in 1913, which is known to have been removed to Rainbow Wood House in 1921. Apart from these there is essentially little change.

Since the 1920s, new buildings have been added, and damage caused during the Second World War has been repaired. Part of the ornamental balustrade and steps in front of St. Paul's had to be completely restored. In 1981, Prior Park College became a co-educational Catholic public school with a lay administration and has now enjoyed over 60 years of occupation as a centre for Catholic secondary education.

In spite of changes to the buildings over the last 250 years, and changes in tree species, the mansion stands majestic on the southern rim overlooking the city of Bath. Ralph Allen's intention of a noble seat "which sees all Bath and is for all Bath to see" is as true today as it was in 1740.[11]

1. Tunstall, Dr. James; *Rambles about Bath*, p. 127 (2nd edition, Simpkin, Marshall and Co., London, 1848).
2. Shepherd; op.cit., p.137.
3. Kilvert, Rev. Francis; *The Diary*, vol. 2, p. 406 (ed. William Plomer, Jonathan Cape, London, 1939).
4. Sale particulars of 15th March 1869, prepared by Cotterell and Spackman, quoted by kind permission of the City of Bristol Record Office, accession number 35721.
5. Seen and quoted by kind permission of the Clifton Diocesan Archivist.
6. Peach; op.cit., p. 242.
7. Shepherd, op.cit.,, p. 102.
8. Little, Bryan; *Prior Park, Its History and Description*, p. 34 (Prior Park College, Bath, 1975).
9. Seen at the Bristol Record Office.
10. Little; op.cit., p. 35.
11. An unnecessarily ironic comment by Philip Thicknesse, quoted in Gadd, David; *Georgian Summer*, p. 86 (Adams and Dart, Bath, 1971).

Epilogue

There is still much that we do not know about the Prior Park landscape, particularly regarding 18th century details, when documentation may have been less than rigorous or plans lost.

We are fortunate, then, in the aspirations of the current occupiers of the estate, Prior Park College. The Trustees of the school are planning a substantial expansion of pupils, facilities and curriculum; at the same time, they are well aware of their responsibilities for the historic buildings and landscape alike. In 1986, the College Trustees, with help from Bath City Council, commissioned a study to identify a strategy for the school's expansion and, among other things, to make proposals for the restoration and management of the historic landscape.

This could lead to the beginning of a third major phase in the life of Prior Park. In particular, it brings the historic landscape into focus and provides an opportunity for further study in order to solve some of the questions which have been posed. With understanding of the intentions of the 18th century creators of the gardens comes the chance to lay the foundations for their restoration and future management.

Bibliography

A number of sources soon became invaluable to me as the ideas for this book transpired. In particular, Benjamin Boyce's thorough biography of Allen, *The Benevolent Man – A Life of Ralph Allen of Bath* (Harvard University Press, Cambridge, Mass., 1967), and the work of another American, Peter Martin, *Pursuing Innocent Pleasures – The Gardening World of Alexander Pope* (Archon Books, Hamden, Connecticut, 1984) which demonstrates the unique contribution of Pope to Prior Park and other gardens of the period. A valuable collection of writings on the subject is to be found in *The Genius of the Place – The English Landscape Garden 1620-1820* (Paul Elek, London, 1975) edited and introduced by John Dixon Hunt and Peter Willis. John Wood's *Essay Towards a Description of Bath* has been published in facsimile (reprinted second edition of 1765, Kingsmead Press, Bath, 1969). The Rev. Monsignor James Shepherd's *Reminiscences of Prior Park* (Isaac Pitman and Sons, London 1894) records the beginnings of the Roman Catholic seminary and there is a thorough history of the College by Rev. Bro. J. S. Roche, *A History of Prior Park College and its Founder Bishop Baines* (Burnes, Oates and Washbourne, London, 1931). The present guidebook for the College, *Prior Park – Its History and Description* by Bryan Little (Prior Park College, Bath, 1975), brings much of the information together.

Further Reading:

Brownell, Morris	*Alexander Pope and the Arts of Georgian England*, Oxford University Press, 1978
Defoe, Daniel	*A Tour through the Whole Island of Great Britain*, London 1724-7; Penguin Books, Harmondsworth, 1971
Fielding, Henry	*Tom Jones*, Andrew Miller, London, 1749; Penguin Books, Harmondsworth, 1966
Gadd, David	*Georgian Summer: Bath in the Eighteenth Century*, Adams and Dart, Bath, 1971
Hadfield, Miles	*A History of British Gardening*, Hutchinson, London, 1960; Penguin Books, Harmondsworth, 1985
Hussey, Christopher	*English Gardens and Landscapes 1700-1750*, Country Life, London 1967
Jones, Richard	*A Life*, transcription of 1858 edition by Mr. Jeffery of Orange Grove in Bath Reference Library
Peach, R. E. M.	*Life and Times of Ralph Allen*, (D. Nutt, London, 1895)
Sherburn, George (ed.)	*Correspondence of Alexander Pope*, Oxford University Press, 4 Vols., 1956
Summerson, Sir John	*Architecture in Britain 1530-1830*, Penguin Books, Harmondsworth, 1953
Tunstall, Dr. James	*Rambles about Bath*, Simpkin, Marshall and Co., London, 1847

Index

Addison, Joseph 32,34
Allen, Philip 61
Allen, Ralph 7,ch.1,ch.2,ch.3,37-39,
    ch.5,ch.6,61,63,75,77

Baines, Bishop 7,45,64-69,73
Bath – Abbey 11,15
    City Council 10,11,77,78
    Population 9,18
    Priory 11,18,19,20,43
Bathampton 15,21
Blenheim 23
Bowood House 54
Boyce, Benjamin 51,53,58
Bramham Park 24-25,27,42
Bridgeman, Charles 24,27,36
Brindle, Thomas 69
Brown, Capability 7,34,54,58-59
Bryant, G.R. 67
Buckeridge, Elizabeth 9,37
Burlington, Lord 23,32-34,37,38,41,47

Calvert, Spackman 76
Campbell, Colen 11,23,25,26,27,57
Cascades 38,44,46,47,48,53,55,63
Castell, Robert 27,33,34
Chandler, Mary 37-38
Chinese influence, 34,57
Chiswick 32,41,47
Cirencester Park 34-35,41,42
Claude le Lorrain 33,57
Clifford, Bishop 72,74,75,76
Cold Bath 48,55
Collinson, John 20,62
Combe Down 11,12,15,17,18,19,21,37
    42,45,62,63,77
Cotterell and Spackman 74
Crewe, Hon. Miss 67
Cunliffe, Barry 18

Dairy House 55
Deer 9,18,20,43
Defoe, Daniel 12,32,45
De Montalt, Baron 63
Dodsley, Isaac 41,43,47
Dolemead 12,62
Dubois, Nicolas 23

Egan, Pierce 63

Farm House 63
Fielding, Henry 51,58
Fishponds 19,45,53,54,56,57,63,71
Fitzmaurice, Francis 62
French influence 27,33,34

Garden Buildings 25,43
Gardener's House 43,47,55,56,67
Goodridge, H.E. 65,66,68,74
Gothic 43,48,55,56,57,58
Gothic Temple 55,56,57,74,77

Grand Tour 23,31
Greenhouse 47,55
Greenwich Hospital 11,15
Grotto 32,36,37,41,43,44,45,47,56,63,
    74,77
Guardian 27,32,34
Gymnasium 68,71,75,76

Hagley Hall 41,58
Hawksmoor, Nicolas 11,25
Hearne, Thomas 17,62
Holder, Elizabeth 37,ch.5,59,61
Hussey, Christophher 25,27

Ice House 56,71
Italian influence 23,25,64

James, John 11,27
Jones, Barbara 44,53
Jones, Inigo 11,23
Jones, Richard 10,29,42,43,52,54,57,
    58,61,65

Kent, William 37,47,48,56,57
King, Austin 19,74
Kitchen Garden 52,55,63

Leland, John 20
Lilliput Avenue 15,37

Martin, Peter 34,36,42,46,48,56
Maude, Cornwallis 63
Miller, Sanderson 58
Monument (Lodge) Field 55,61
Moses, statue of 45,46,47,48

Naturalism 24,27,31,32,34,36,44,49,
    51,52,55
Nostell Priory 25

Oswald, Arthur 24
Overton, John 43,45,54,55,56,57

Padmore, John 12
Palladian Bridge 53-55,59,63
Palladianism 12,15,23,24,25,26,27,31
    34,41,54,57
Parterre 24,27,31,34
Peach, R.E.M.43,75
Picturesque 27,58
Pineapples 45,47,55
Pitt, William 20,54,58,59
Pliny 33
Pococke, Richard 46,48
Pope, Alexander 7,27,ch.4,ch.5,52,
    53,54,56
Postal service 9,10,11,15,37,61
Potter Thomas 20,54
Poussin, Nicholas 33,57
Priory 66,67,76
Priory Cottage 63

Quarries 11,12,15,17,18,21,37,38,45,
    62,63,68,75,77
Railway 12
Rainbow Wood 61,77
Ralph Allen Drive 12,42,77
Repton, Humphrey 34,54
Richardson, Samuel 45,46,51
Robins, Thomas 53,54
Roche, J.S. 68,73
Rock Gate 57
Roman Catholicism 64-65,72,76,77
Roman influence 9,15,18,23,25,27,33
Rousham 27,34,36,47,48

St. Batholomew's Hospital 15
St. Paul's House 65,72,77
St. Peter's House 65,67,68
Scoles, Joseph 69,73
Scot, Henry 47
Serle, John 34,44,47
Serpentine 37,47,48,49,55,75
Sham Bridge 48,55
Sham Castle 55,58
Shenstone, William 32
Shepherd, James 63,65-68,72,75
Sherborne Castle 34,36,47,48
Spence, Joseph 33,34
Stourhead 27
Stowe 34,36,37,58
Summerson, Sir John 23,25,56
Switzer, Stephen 24

Temple, Sir Wiilliam 34
Terraces 17,42,45,65,67,71,76
Thatch'd House 55,56
Thomas, John 63
Thompson, Thomas 72,75,76
Thorp, Thomas 21,37,42,43,45,47,51
    53,54,55,56,57
Tunstall, James 7,71
Twickenham 32,34,41,44,45,53

Vanburgh, Sir John 23,25

Wade, George 9,10,11,42-43,63
Walker, Anthony 12,51,52,53,55
Walpole, Horace 31,32,49,57
Wanstead House 25,29
Warburton family 43,53,54,59,61,62,6?
Water 24,27,29,31,36,37,38,41,42,45,
    46,49,51,52,54,67
Wentworth Woodhouse 25-26
Whiggism 23,25
Widcombe 11,17,18,19,21,37,39,41,46,77
Williams, Edward 72,76
Wilton House 54
Wood, John 7,11,15,17,18,ch.3,41,51,
    52,54,65,69,73
Wren, Sir Christopher 23,56
Wroxton 57